What People Are Saying...

"Baker has taken a topic that makes me break out in a rash, made me laugh and forget my itch. I couldn't wait to read more."

—JD Rogers, Editor, *The Applegator*—a newspaper dealing with rural resource issues in southern Oregon.

"As a poison ivy researcher for almost thirty years, I feel the author has done a great job researching the subject. Valuable information on the plants identification, control, treatment options, and a good lesson on the immune system. A must-read book if you have any interest in or encounter with poison ivy/oak or poison sumac."

—Mahmoud A. ElSohly, Ph.D. Research Professor, Research Inst. of Pharmaceutical Sciences. Nat. Center for Natural Products Research. University of MS.

"This book is written in a casual, lighthearted style, but is very comprehensive and informative, especially for the lay person."

—Bettye H. Galloway. Executive Vice President (ret). ElSohly Laboratories, Inc (ELI)

"The chapter on identifying poison oak and poison ivy is worth the price of the book alone."

—Jeff Renfrow, Biologist, River-Rafting Guide

"The author has distilled every facet of knowledge concerning these ubiquitous plants and their kin into a marvelous volume of botanical lore, medical fact and practical advice. You will never look at these itch-inducing plants in quite the same way."

—Alan W. Meerow, Ph.D., Research plant geneticist and systematist, USDA-Agricultural Research Service

"Who knew poison oak/ivy could be so interesting and fun...to read about anyway. You'll want to read from cover to cover."

—Tony Baker, native plant landscaper, naturalist

D1562443

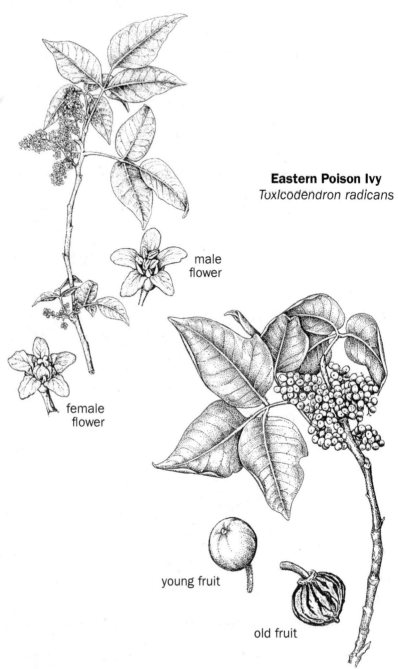

Eastern Poison Ivy
Toxicodendron radicans

male
flower

female
flower

young fruit

old fruit

Reprinted with permission from Rhodora 73: 143-144
(1971). Illustration by Priscilla Fawcett.

THE POISON OAK & POISON IVY SURVIVAL GUIDE

A RASH-TAMING, MYSTERY-SOLVING ROMP THROUGH THESE AMAZING PLANTS

Sandra J. Baker

Coleman
Creek
Press

Medford, OR

THE POISON OAK & POISON IVY SURVIVAL GUIDE
A RASH-TAMING, MYSTERY-SOLVING ROMP THROUGH THESE AMAZING PLANTS

MEDICAL DISCLAIMER
This book is intended as an informational guide only. The remedies and approaches described herein are not meant to be a substitute for professional medical care or treatment. They should not be used to treat a serious ailment without prior consultation with a qualified healthcare professional.

Cover drawing and interior drawings: Dan Paine
Cover design and typesetting: Align Visual Arts & Communication
Editing: Barbara Holliday

www.poisonoakandpoisonivy.com

ISBN 978-0-9833706-0-4

Coleman Creek Press
6454 Coleman Ck. Rd.
Medford OR 97501

colemancreekpress@opendoor.com

Printed in the U.S.

TABLE OF CONTENTS

ACKNOWLEDGEMENTS

Thank you to the many folks who took time to share their knowledge. You all added something to this book.

A special thank you to the many experts in their fields—chemistry, botany, allergy immunology, etc.—who looked over chapters for errors or gave me important information: Curt Beebe, Donald G. Crosby, Edward M. Kerwin, Mahmoud A. ElSohly, Vera Byers, Jean H. Langenheim, Jun Wen, Susan Pell, Shelly Lotz.

My son John and daughter Diane humored me by looking over rough drafts, thinking it was a weekend hobby that probably wouldn't go very far.

My son Dan contributed much with his cartoons and plant drawings. Working together was a comedy of miscommunication—by e-mail, phone, and even when sitting next to each other.

My cousin Barbara Sommer was able to obtain most of the clinical studies I needed, and as a long time college professor, she had no mercy when red penciling early drafts.

And finally, my gratitude to my husband David who patiently trotted off to work for three years while I insisted I was writing all that time. He was once heard wistfully muttering, "I wonder when I'll get my wife back."

INTRODUCTION

After reading my book, you may discover you learned more about poison oak and poison ivy than you ever thought possible. During a hike with friends, you might suddenly stop short and exclaim, "Great Scott, it's *Toxicodendron diversiloba*. Stand back."

Many physicians advise us just to put up with a case of poison oak or poison ivy. It seems there aren't many drugs available besides corticosteroids, which may or may not work, and you will not know which—for days. They prescribe medication to soothe the itch, and still we suffer. We become our own nurses, while we deal with an affliction that demands constant attention—applying potions, soaking in herbal baths, and changing dressings throughout the long days and endless nights. We slowly retreat into our own universe of horrible itching, pushing others away, mumbling "Don't touch me."

In our pitiful attempts to self-medicate, desperation has fueled the application of weird and sometimes dangerous substances. Here are a few: crawfish, gasoline, gunpowder, meat tenderizer, and even urine (preferably your own, but horse urine is acceptable. You will need a large bucket and plenty of patience).

HELP IS ON THE WAY. Relax, mark pages, make notes, and have fun while you learn about poison oak and ivy and how to deal with the consequences of accidental contact with their strong allergenic oil.

ONE DAY MANY YEARS AGO, I strolled into a hospital research library seeking articles on poison oak and poison ivy for a small book I was writing. Hearing my request, the attendant quietly snipped that she considered a poison oak or poison ivy rash a minor affliction compared to the serious conditions usually researched by the hospital's physicians.

Obviously she herself had never experienced a bad case of poison oak or poison ivy.

The following are comments from some of those afflicted by a condition that really is not that minor.

"I literally wanted to jump out of my skin."

"It was horrible."

"My face looked so awful I scared my children."

"I was nearly insane."

"The swelling was so bad I didn't recognize myself in the mirror."

"I was in absolute agony."

"My right forearm looked like a horror-movie prop."

"I couldn't even stand still."

"I spent four days in the hospital."

One of the most adventurous of poison ivy researchers, Albert Kligman, dramatically wrote in 1958, "The victim is seized with a wild maniacal itching, which liquefies the hardiest will and shatters the spirit."[1]

FOR TWO DECADES, my home was a small farm in the mountains of Santa Cruz, California. I cut wood in the forest while the dogs and horses ambled through acres of poison oak plants. I carried the wood, hugged the animals, and wondered why poison oak rashes kept popping up all over my skin.

A year went by before it dawned on me that my poison oak rashes were never completely healed before another rash would pop up to take its place—over and over again. Usually the rash was small—no big deal. Every once in a while, though, it was terrible. My body became a perpetual-motion itching machine. I suffered for years until one day it seemed I wasn't reacting as often or as badly. As time passed, I itched less and less. I had the impression I was losing my sensitivity to the oil even though I still barreled through patches of poison oak to cut firewood and continued to snuggle my animals.

My interest in poison oak grew, so in 1979 I self-published a small book on poison oak and poison ivy.[2] Since leaving our little farm, my husband and I have lived in five country homes—each one surrounded by poison oak. It seems to be my destiny. I decided it was about time I really researched the subject. So here you are.

References

1. Kligman, Albert M. 1958. "Cashew Nut Shell Oil for Hyposensitization against Rhus Dermatitis." *AMA Arch Derm* 78(3).

2. Baker, Sandra J. 1979. *Poison Oak and Poison Ivy. Why It Itches, What To Do.* Soquel, CA.

Western Poison Oak
Toxicodendron diversilobum

Eastern Poison Ivy
Toxicodendron radicans

Western Poison Ivy
Toxicodendron rydbergii

Eastern Poison Oak
Toxicodendron pubescens

Poison Sumac
Toxicodendron vernix

Chapter 1

IDENTIFYING POISON OAK & POISON IVY

THE POISON OAK & POISON IVY IDENTIFICATION SYSTEM
Leaves of three, let it be.

This scene is played out every spring, summer, and fall. Someone will yell out, "STOP! Three leaves! Don't go any closer!"

Three leaves hanging around together seem to get everyone in a dither. Want to know if you really should worry?

Take a deep breath and walk up close to the plant. Yep, real close. Solve each clue before you go on to the next.

1. Leaves

   a. Start at the **very end** of one branch. Do you see three leaves grouped together?

   Good. Now look at the rest of the leaves.

   1. Are *single* leaves growing up the rest of the branch instead of groupings?

   If so, this plant is out of the running. (You saw the last leaf at the tip of a branch and thought it was part of a threesome).

2. Or, do you see groupings of three leaves all the way up the branch? If so, this plant is possibly poison oak or poison ivy.

No—3 leaves grouped at tip of branch but not elsewhere

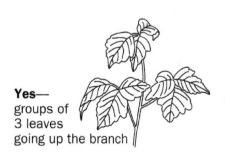

Yes— groups of 3 leaves going up the branch

b. Okay, lets say you definitely have groupings of three leaves going up the branch.

There are a couple of possibilities.

l. The stems of the three leaves could be joined together on one main stem, creating *one* leaf.

- Botanically, each of the three is now called a *leaflet.*

- Poison oak and poison ivy, plus some other plants, fall into this category).

2. But, you also might be looking at groupings of three single leaves that happen to be in close proximity to one another. These are out of the running.

At this point we will assume you are looking at three leaflets on one stem.

2. Leaflets

a. Look at the *middle* leaflet. Its stem should be longer than the stem of the two side leaflets. It might be slightly longer or much longer, but it will never be the same length or shorter.

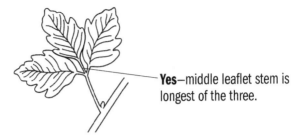

Yes—middle leaflet stem is longest of the three.

b. Check out the two side leaflets. They should have short stems in relation to the stem of the middle leaflet.

Yes—short leaflet stem (often almost too short to detect)

c. If all three leaflets seem to be missing stems, this is *not* poison oak or poison ivy.

No—leaflet stems are absent

3. Leaflet veins

Find the main vein of a leaflet. There will be side veins. A side vein will not be directly across from another side vein. They are in alternate positions off the main vein.

Yes—alternate side veins

No—veins are across from each other

4. Leaf stem

• Each leaf stem (remember it has three leaflets attached) has a distinctive base, which is slightly thickened and shaped in a curve like a celery stalk. It might or might not have a bud or new leaf stem at the base. Stems are very small, and this clue is hard to see.

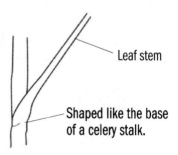

Leaf stem

Shaped like the base of a celery stalk.

5. Leaf placement on branch

• Once you have identified the leaf stem, study the placement on the branch in relation to the other leaf stems.

• Just like the veins, no leaf stem is directly across from another. This is called an *alternate* leaf pattern.

• Some plants have an *opposite* leaf pattern (leaves are directly across from each other), which puts them out of the running.

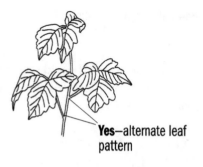

Yes–alternate leaf pattern

No–stems are directly across from one another

6. Flowers

• You might spot hanging clumps of tiny white flowers.

• Flowers grow alternately on flower stems just as leaves do on branches.

• Female and male plants produce flowers, which may or may not be fragrant. If so, the scent is lovely.

7. Fruit

• The fruit (drupes) are round and light green when young.

• Ripened fruit is white or cream and looks like a tiny peeled orange with a thin black line between the segments, an effect that is quite distinctive even if a bit small, being of lesser diameter than a pea.

• Later the fruit looks a bit shriveled; not as distinctive as when plump.

• Fruits hang in small, messy-looking clumps on stiff stems. *Only female plants* (having been pollinated by male flowers) *produce fruit.*

There is an alternating pattern you may have noticed—alternating leaflet veins off main vein, alternating leaf stems on branch, alternating flowers on flower stem (then the fruit).

8. Pitch-black resin spots

• Check a number of leaflets for *tiny* pitch-black spots where bruising or insects have punctured resin ducts. Like a leaky pipe, a bit of clear or milky resin has seeped to the surface, turned black and hardened.

• Sometimes there are many black spots on a leaflet, but usually there are none. Check stems, branches and trunks.

• Large pitch-black splotches on trunks and branches indicate that a deep wound in the bark was sealed with resin; a positive identification.

Black resin spots. There might be many or none.

Black resin sealing wound in bark.

9. Forcing resin out

• Another means of identification, if you have time to spare, is to place a small stem between two sheets of white paper.

• Crush the stem with a stone, freeing the resin. Shortly—maybe in twenty minutes—the resin will turn dark yellow. In an hour it probably will have turned brown. By twenty-four hours there is a good chance it will have hardened and turned black.. The timing can vary, depending on humidity and temperature.

• Cutting into the bark of a trunk will also bring forth the resin. If you have a magnifying glass handy, slice a stem and observe the resin ducts arranged like numbers on a clock.

• The emerging resin will later turn the cut end black, except maybe during fall or winter when there is less resin.

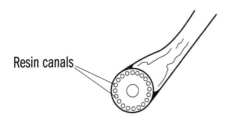

Resin canals

Now look at the *whole* plant. **The plants can grow either as ground-crawling vines, short bushes, tall bushes or vines growing up a tree or post.**

10. Vine growth

• A suspicious vine is climbing up a tree and you can't see the leaves, which are often out of view as they attempt to breach the canopy.

• This part is easy: Does the trunk twine like a barber pole? If so, it is *not* poison oak or poison ivy, which, if in a climbing mood, grows almost straight up because the trunk either leans against something or is held against the host by its aerial roots (aboveground roots on the trunk).

• If there is a bush nearby, the vines might fall over the bush and use it for support, growing almost horizontally, while the tips of the stems have a distinctive slight upward curve.

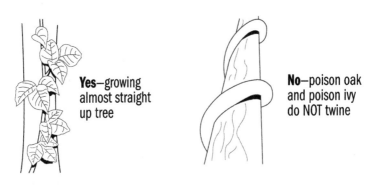

Yes—growing almost straight up tree

No—poison oak and poison ivy do NOT twine

11. Aerial roots

• Eastern poison ivy tends to grow prolific grasping (aerial) roots on mature vines and can resemble a beat-up old rope, a strong identifier.

• If a western poison oak vine grows aerial roots, they are short, sparse and barely noticeable.

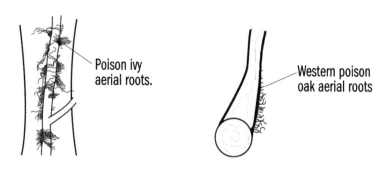

Poison ivy aerial roots.

Western poison oak aerial roots

12. Stems

• There are no wispy endings to these plants.

• When you brush against a stem you will feel resistance.

13. Bark

• Bark is smooth red-brown on new wood, becoming gray-brown and weathered gray on older wood (often covered with lichen).

14. Fall colors

• One sees a full range of bright fall colors, although plants in dry, sunny meadows may simply turn tan and dry up.

BELOW IS THE SAME INFORMATION IN A CONCENTRAT-ED FORM. IF YOU CAN IDENTIFY POISON OAK OR POISON IVY WITH THIS, YOU ARE ON YOUR WAY.

Remember the alternating pattern you learned.

1. Leaves

• Three leaflets on one leaf stem, continuing up the branch in sets of three.

  • More than three leaflets is possible, but not probable (especially western poison oak).

2. Leaflets

  • The middle leaflet will have a longer stem than the other two.

  • The other two leaflets will have short stems.

3. Leaflet veins

  • Side veins of a leaflet are placed alternately off the main vein.

4. Leaf stem

  • Base is thickened, like a celery stalk.

5. Leaf placement on branch

  • Alternate pattern, not across from each other.

6. Flowers

  • Tiny, white and hang in clusters. May or may not be fragrant.

  • Flowers alternate on flower stem.

7. Fruit

  • Smaller than a pea. Light green when young; white when ripe, resembling a tiny peeled orange. Black stripes between segments.

8. Pitch-black resin spots

  • Search on leaves, stems and trunks.

9. Forcing resin out:

• Crush stem for definite identification. Will probably take hours to turn black. Caution encouraged.

10. Vine growth

• Almost straight up, no barber-pole twining. Parts of the plant sometimes lay over bushes with the tips curving upward.

11. Aerial roots (help the vine climb by grasping host)

• Older eastern poison ivy vines resemble old ropes. Western poison oak aerial roots will be absent or not obvious.

12. Stems

• Strong and flexible. No wimpy thin stems.

13. Bark

• Old weathered grey to newer smooth red-brown.

14. Fall colors

• Variable, from dull to bright.

WINTER IDENTIFICATION

When you develop a feel for the winter look, identification can be easier than in other seasons.

1. Leaves will have dropped, leaving a raised U or V-shaped scar, where the leaf stem was attached. This is very distinctive. Scars will alternate on the stem rather than being across from each other.

2. During winter, languid-looking vines draped over sturdy shrubs are typical, as is the gentle curve of the tip toward the sun. Notice the short side stems growing alternately up the larger stems, and the small pointed buds on their tips.

3. Without leaves, trunks and stems are easily observed. As your eyes move back from the tip of a stem, the smooth wood will become grayer. Lichen and moss may be present and the wood begins to look old and weathered.

4. Short shrubs in meadows are a bit harder to identify. Leaf scars get you on the right track. You will notice multiple branches growing upward, but without the here-and-there branching style of most shrubs. Instead, short side shoots are placed alternatively on each branch in a tidy way.

5. In balmy Southern California, leaves may not drop during the winter.

WHAT YOU WILL *NEVER* SEE ON POISON OAK OR POISON IVY PLANTS

- Flowers growing from the end of a stem.
- Single large flowers.
- Flowers any color other than cream or white.
- Upright flowers.
- Fruit larger than a pea.
- Red, blue or purple fruit.
- Leaf stalks directly across from each other on the stem.
- Sharp spines.
- A vine twining like a barber pole.

OTHER VARIETIES OF *TOXICODENDRONS* WITH THEIR OWN IDIOSYNCRASIES

Eastern poison oak. *Toxicodendron pubescens*

- Does not grow as a vine. Has the characteristics of a poison oak shrub form.
- Leaves are often covered with short, downy hairs, giving the plant a velvety look. This is a variable trait.
- Grows on barren, gravelly soil in the southeast.

Western poison ivy. *Toxicodendron rydbergii*

- Has the characteristics of a poison ivy shrub form. May grow up to ten feet, but is usually no taller than three feet, with only a single stem.

• The leaflets fold upward at the rib like a butterfly. This is a variable trait.

Poison Sumac. *Toxicodendron vernix*

• The leaflet midrib is red.

• Likes marshes. Regular sumacs cannot survive in water.

• There are four to seven sets of leaflets per stem with a leaflet at the end.

• White flowers, white berries.

• Leaflets have smooth edges and are shaped like rabbits ears three to four inches long.

• The sumacs it resembles have red flowers and red berries, and sawtooth leaves or a winged leaf stalk between the leaf sets.

PLANTS THAT RESEMBLE POISON OAK AND POISON IVY

Virginia creeper. *Parthenocissus quinquefolia:* This plant is often mentioned as a poison ivy look-alike. Not so. Virginia creeper has *five* leaflets, not three. It has aerial roots, but they have flat adhesive discs at the end, very different from poison ivy's short, fuzzy aerial roots. Virginia creeper also has purple berries.

Box elder. *Acer negundo:* Called the most common look-alike for poison ivy, the pictures certainly resemble the plants. This is a tree; consequently, only small saplings will look suspicious. Yes, it has three leaflets per leaf, but *the leaf stems are directly across from each other on the branch.* Case closed. You don't even need to know what this plant is; you now know what it is not.

Wafer ash. *Ptelea trifoliata:* This shrub or tree resembles the box elder. There are three leaflets per stem, but there is no little stem at the end of *any* of the three leaflets.

Bladdernut. *Staphylea trifolia:* The leaves are *opposite* on the stem. Poison oak and poison ivy are *alternate* on the stem.

Boston ivy, English ivy. *Parthenocissus family:* These plants have good examples of aerial roots. If you spot an ivy vine growing up a tree, take note for future reference: the two ivies have single leaves, not three leaflets per leaf stem.

Wild grape. *Vitis:* Leaves are arranged alternately along the stem like poison oak and poison ivy, but they are *single* leaves instead of three leaflets per leaf stem. Besides, these are weak vines with tendrils.

Wild blackberry. This plant is covered in sharp spines.

Aromatic sumac. *Rhus aromatica:* Very similar in appearance to poison oak and poison ivy. My daughter has this gorgeous plant and was worried, but it is too perfect—a lush bush, neat and tidy. One big tip-off is that the leaves have an aromatic scent when crushed.

Botanical description of *Toxicodendrons*

"Trees, shrubs and vines. Leaves alternate, trifoliolate, multifoliolate (rarely unifoliolate). Inflorescences pendent, axillary panicles. Flowers: male and female flowers on separate individuals (dioecious; perianths pentamerous; disk intrastaminal, five-lobed; stamens five; ovary unilocular, the ovule basal, the style one, the stigma one. Drupe exocarp separates from mesocarp when ripe."[1]

Now you should be able to identify the plants in all their incarnations. Poison oak and poison ivy can be long and lanky, short and squat, limp and laying, upright and stiff, a dull dried-out hue or dressed for Mardi Gras.

HISTORICAL RHYMES

(leaves changed to *leaflets* for botanical accuracy)

Leaflets three, let it be; leaflets five, let it thrive.

Berries red, have no dread; berries white, a poisonous sight.

Hairy vine, no friend of mine. (poison ivy vines)

Raggy rope, don't be a dope. (poison ivy vines)

Red leaves in the spring, it's a dangerous thing.

Side leaves like mittens, will itch like the dickens. (Eastern poison oak)

DEVELOPING A POISON OAK & POISON IVY AUTOMATIC SENSOR™
Type of people who venture into poison oak and poison ivy country

1. THE BLISSFULLY IGNORANT

Never having been in poison oak or poison ivy country before, the Blissfully Ignorant haven't a clue. They sometimes wade through thickets of the plants to pick lovely bouquets of its colorful fall leaves. There is nothing to say—most are doomed.

2. THE HOPELESSLY IGNORANT

Their refrain is "What, me worry? I don't get it." That is, until the day they do—head to toe. This is rather embarrassing to someone whose identity is attached to being the only person in the group who never gets the cursed rash. Members of this clique may suddenly decide that big cities have all they will ever need in life, or they develop a newfound interest in plant identification and join group number three, "The Enthusiastic Newcomer."

3. THE ENTHUSIASTIC NEWCOMER

These folks are learning to identify the plants, yet they still have trouble distinguishing between poison oak and berry vines. They helpfully shout "EGADS—POISON IVY. DON'T GO THERE. GOOD GRAVY—YOU'RE STANDING RIGHT IN IT," and so forth.

4. DEVELOPING A POISON OAK AND POISON IVY AUTOMATIC SENSOR

After a few years of tripping cluelessly over poison oak, I finally made it into this group. We have nudged it, waded through it, fallen in it, pulled it up and dug it up. Once I even sprayed cut stems and leaves (consequently the resin) all over my barelegged and tank-topped body while cutting what looked like harmless brush with my chain saw.

As we finish the first stages in our encounters with poison oak or poison ivy, we head into this last category. When we bushwhack, we instinctively look ahead. We slide our hips to the left, take an extra hop to the right, duck our heads, and don't really notice what we just did, other than walk along and enjoy our hike. As we approach a bare vine needing to be pushed out of the way, we automatically raise our eyes up the vine, searching for what the leaves at the top look like.

I have a piece of a newsletter from the eighties. The author says she has a small computer in her head with an "automatic recognition and avoidance response." Same thing, different words. (In the article, she happens to mention that the booklet on poison oak and poison ivy I wrote in 1979 is, ahem, "...the best presentation I've seen.")

So, take your knocks, read the other chapters, continue to tramp through poison oak or poison ivy for years, and then—one spring, without even noticing, you will have a Poison Oak & Poison Ivy Automatic Sensor. At this point, your "sensor" will notice all forms of poison oak or poison ivy because your brain will have captured the essence of the plant, the little nuances of its personality.

References

1. Mitchell, John D. "The Poisonous Anacardiaceae Genera of the World." Pages 103-129 in the G.T. Prance & M.J. Balick (eds.), *New Directions in the Study of Plants and People*. Quote permission by Advances in Economic Botany, Vol. 8. © 1990, The New York Botanical Garden Press, Bronx, New York.

Chapter 2

ALL
ABOUT
THE
PLANTS

BOTANICAL CLASSIFICATION
(Why they have complicated names)

If you and I, strolling along in the Oregon countryside, met up with a Western poison oak plant and I was in a formal mood, I would say, "I am so pleased to introduce you to *Toxicodendron diversilobum*. Toxi, I would like you to meet . . . "

Western poison oak is known internationally by its formal name because of a system that identifies all living things (a type of information filing system). These names are in Latin. The botanical classification places plants in groups with each group having more in common with each other until, near the end, each separate plant is named and shares many characteristics with the other named plants it typically interbreeds with—in the grouping called species.

Let us work our way down the plant side of the "Classification of Living Organisms" to where it meets *Toxicodendron*. I am using the chart from the U.S. Dept. of Agriculture.[1]

Kingdom: *Plantae.*

Phylum: (Sometimes called "Division"): *Magnoliophyta.*

Class: *Magnollopsida.* The English word "dicotyledon" is often
used. (Subclass: *Rosidae*).

Order: *Sapindales.*

Family: *Anacardiaceae.* Called the cashew family,
or sumac family. There are 82 genera and
approximately 800 species.[2] More skin reactions
come from this family then from all other
families combined.[3]

Genus: *Toxicodendron.* (Means "poisonous tree.").
Certain members of *Anacardiaceae* were
moved from *Rhus* into this, their own genus.

**There are four sections of *Toxicodendron* based upon growth
forms.**[4]

1. Toxicodendron **section:** Woody vines or shrubs, with three
   leaflets per leaf stem (generally).
   (Those underlined are found in the United States.)
   Species:
   T. diversilobum: Western (also called Pacific) poison oak.
   U.S., Canada, Mexico (Baja).
   T. pubescens: Eastern (also called Atlantic) poison oak. U.S.
   T. rydbergii: Western poison ivy. U.S. Canada (considered
   by some botanists to only be a subspecies
   of *T. radicans*)
   T. radicans: Eastern poison ivy. U.S., Canada.
   Sub species (these are basically eastern poison ivy, but
   have individual variations and distinctive geographical
   ranges.[4] Any *T. radicans* you spot will be one of the
   following sub species).
   ssp. *barkley*: Mexico, Guatemala.
   ssp. *divaricatum*: S.E. corner of Arizona, Mexico.

ssp. *eximium*: S.W. Texas, Mexico.

ssp. *hispidum*: China, Taiwan, Japan.

ssp. *negundo*: Great Lake states, central states, and
    Midwest. Southern lobe of Ontario, Canada.

ssp. *orientale*: Japan.

ssp. *pubens*: Mississippi valley.

ssp. *radicans*: Eastern and south-eastern U.S., Bermuda,
    Bahamas' Islands, Nova Scotia.

ssp. *verrucosum*: Texas, Oklahoma.

2. Venanata section: Tree-like growth.

Species:

T. vernix: poison sumac. U.S.

T. vernicifluum: Japanese lacquer tree. China, Japan, Korea,
    India.

T. succedaneum: wax tree, Japanese Wax tree. Japan, India.

T. nodosum: Indonesia, Malaysia.

T. trichocarpum: China, Japan, Korea.

T. sylvestre: China, Japan, Korea, Taiwan.

T. delavayi: China.

T. yunnanense: China.

T. grandeflorum: China.

3. Griffithii section: Similar to venenata section, but with thick
leather like leaves and differences in fruit.

Species:

T. striatum: Central America, Northern South America.

T. griffithii: China.

T. fulvum: China, Thailand.

T. wallichii: China, India, Nepal.

T. hookrti: China, India.

4. Simplifolia section: Single leaf on a leaf stem.

Species:

T. borneense: Borneo.

In school I learned this handy little ditty to help remember the chart headings (from kingdom to species): **K**ing **P**hillip **C**ome **O**ut **F**or **G**ods **S**ake. It has hovered in my brain since 1978 and refuses to leave.

This all sounds very simple doesn't it? Just slot a plant in where it goes. Except that people keep trying to "fix" the chart. New information is discovered, or something doesn't make sense. Modern inventions have allowed better views into plant tissues, and computers have helped organize the taxonomic systems.

Poison oak, poison ivy and poison sumac were once placed with the sumacs (*Rhus*). In the 1930s, it was decided to create another genus *Toxicodendron*, meaning "poisonous tree." This change remained controversial. W. T. Gillis was a highly respected botanist who pushed for *Toxicodendron* as a separate genus due to these five unique characteristics:

1. Presence of urushiol (the allergenic oil).
2. An absence of red glandular hairs on fruits and pedicels (leaf stalk).
3. Pollen size (significantly smaller and often more round than those of Rhus).
4. Hanging flowers.
5. Color of fruit (cream or white).[4]

Even though the name has changed from *Rhus*, the rash from these plants is sometimes called *Rhus* Dermatitis. Homeopathic dilutions of poison ivy are still being sold as *Rhus* tox, from the old name for poison ivy *Rhus toxicodendron*.

After "Family" in the chart, things start getting messy. "Sections", "Sub-species" and "tribes" are planted here and there. I tried to sort it out, but something will probably be changed before the ink is dry from the printer. According to Donald Crosby in his book *The Poisoned Weed*,[5] eastern poison ivy has had its botanical name changed at least fifty times. Western poison oak had around fourteen changes, and botanists are still quibbling. Luckily the International Code of Botanical Nomenclature has very stringent rules for assigning names.

Now I am done with the Biological Classification Chart. It drove me crazy. No two pieces of research were the same. I rest my case for being so flippant, with the following quote from the Angiosperm Phylogeny Group, composed of experts in the field. "No classification is ever final; it presents a view at a particular point in time, based on a particular state of research. New results are always appearing."[6] And with *Toxicodendron* in particular, biologist David Senchina wrote, "The taxonomy of *Toxicodendron* has been in flux throughout the twentieth century, and is still being amended."[7]

Western Poison Oak
Toxicodendron diversilobum

An example of leaflets without
deep scallops.

BOTANY OF POISON OAK AND POISON IVY
(Leaves, Flowers, Fruit, Resin)

Toxicodendron diversiloba: Western poison oak (also called Pacific poison oak)

Toxicodendron radicans: Eastern poison ivy

Toxicodendron pubescens: Eastern poison oak (also called Atlantic poison oak)

Toxicodendron rydbergii: Western poison ivy

These four species in the genus *Toxicodendron* have been given many common names throughout the years. "Western poison oak" and "eastern poison oak" are commonly used, although some researchers prefer using Pacific and Atlantic respectively. I find that I become mixed up when I use so many terms for the west and east coasts, so I will stick to western and eastern.

The top two plants on this page, western poison oak and eastern poison ivy, are what most folks mean when they say "poison oak" or "poison ivy." The two other species, western poison ivy and eastern poison oak, each have some distinctive characteristics and growth habits that I will describe later in the chapter.

Why are these plants so hard to spot?

Poison oak and poison ivy are like that guy you know who one day has long hair, the next day a buzz cut. Then he grows a mustache, later a full beard. You know him well, but he seems different each time you see him. One day you might walk right by him in the street.

They easily grow in various environments, from a sunny, dry meadow to the darker, damp forest. You will find them from sea level on up to five thousand feet or so.

Climbing into a small dead tree, they eagerly spread out. The tree appears alive, if a bit straggly.

When lacking support to climb, they grow shrub-like in the sun, or trail along the ground, blending in with other forest layabouts.

As kids run through the dry, brown grass of a winter meadow, certain leafless stems whip against bare legs. A couple of days later, strange two-inch-long welts appear.

The leaves blend in so well with the old bush that needed trimming that the rash will come as a complete surprise.

Besides individual species having differences in growth habits, each of the four species of *Toxicodendrons* can be variable from plant to plant, and even variable on an individual plant. *There are no absolutes when describing poison oak and poison ivy.*

LEAVES

There is an old saying, "Leaves of three, let it be. Leaves of five, let it thrive." It was always comforting to believe that if a plant did not have three leaves (called "leaflets") grouped together, we were safe, safe, safe. Well...not always.

One leaf is comprised of three separate leaflets with scalloped, toothed or lobed edges. This group is attached to a stem (petiole), which is attached to a larger stem or branch.

To reiterate, *each set of three leaflets is one leaf.* Although very uncommon, there have been sightings among western poison oaks of four to seven leaflets on a single leaf stem. Once, a group of plants with up to 17 leaflets per leaf stem was spotted by William Gillis, a well-known botanist.[8] Curt Beebe of northern California, who has spent years studying poison oak in the field, says it takes 15 to 20 minutes of gazing at a patch of poison oak plants, rather high up, above eye level, to spot leaves composed of more than three leaflets. They grow near the tips of stems, and can be scattered on one plant.[9]

The leaflets themselves are hard to describe—they come in a multitude of shapes and sizes, from oval with pointed tips, to scalloped or lobed with rounded tips.

The green or reddish-bronze spring leaves have a fresh, shiny glow. As the leaves develop they wear various hues of green. Those in the shade might be a bit lighter, larger and thinner than leaves in the sun. In drier meadows where the hot sun beats down, leaves dry out and become tan or dull yellow toward the end of summer, whereas leaves in the shade keep their green color longer, even into the fall. The wonderful fall colors seem the most vibrant in the fringe areas between forest and meadow.

Every so often, leaves have pouch-like reddish growths called galls, created by the plant after gall mites have laid their eggs in the plant tissue.[10] A rare phenomenon called "fasciation galls" (which I called "fascination" for two weeks until I discovered my eyes had deceived me), is formed from terminal leaflets that fan out and create interesting shapes resembling elk or moose antlers. Mites or fungi are possible culprits, but the cause is not known for certain.

As fall progresses, leaves turn combinations of bright yellow, orange, pink and red. The resin of the plant containing the allergen urushiol is drawn back from the leaves into the stems. If a leaf had never been damaged, supposedly it would no longer contain urushiol and you would be able to blow your nose in it without worries. But most leaves have been munched by insects or chewed by animals, ending up a bit battered. Sap leaking to the surface of the leaf, creating small, shiny black spots, will have hardened, but still might give you a wallop of a rash.

Poison oak and poison ivy are said to lose their leaves in winter, but while walking in the southern Californian city of Claremont, Donald Crosby, author of *The Poisoned Weed*, observed huge western poison oak plants in full leaf during the middle of winter.[17]

FLOWERS

The tiny five-petal flowers are greenish-white or light yellow, and are grouped in hanging clusters (inflorescences). They appear in early summer. New plants are destined to be male or female. The pollen from a male (staminate) flower needs to reach the ovary of the female (pistillate) flower before the ovary turns from white to black, or "too late Jack." Like humans, a male plant will never have babies (fruit). Sometimes though, a female plant will produce male flowers along with female flowers, although fertility of these is variable. This plant is then called a hermaphrodite. Looking at it in human terms, she feels her eggs were not pollinated sufficiently and goes by the philosophy, "If you want something done right, do it yourself."

It's not as though these plants are hard to pollinate. Bees love the flowers. The "flat face and radical symmetry are attractive to insects." Dedicated poison ivy flower watchers have noted various flies, wasps, ants, beetles, butterflies and hemiptera wandering about the flowers.[11] And the stickiness of the pollen holds it to the flower—you will not find any blowing in the wind.

If you are a curious person, you will want to get really close to smell the sweet perfume. When my nose is about four inches away, I smell a jasmine-like fragrance, but some folks cannot detect a scent. It seems to be a variable trait. You can check out the differences between the tiny male and female flowers with a magnifying glass. Look into the center of the flower. The female will have an enlargement, the pistil (containing the ovary), which resembles a bulb-like growth. This separates into three parts at the end, the stigmas. If instead you see five tiny stems (stamens) with enlarged tips (anthers) painted a gaudy orange—signaling, "Here, I'm over here"—this is a male flower. They produce pollen, the carrier of the sperm. Bees carry the pollen from the stamens to the female flowers. When a pollen grain lands on the stigma of the female flower, it grows a tube down into the ovary. The sperm is shot toward the waiting egg, and there you have it—fertilization. This all seems vaguely familiar doesn't it? Then a baby, I mean, a berry begins to form.

As the male flowers begin to die, their job done, new single mothers are raising families of cute little drupes.

FRUIT (Drupes)

"Berries white, a poisonous sight. Berries red, have no dread." This little mantra is true, except that you may not notice the small, nondescript fruit blending in with the leaves.

Botanically, a poison oak and poison ivy fruit is called a drupe, which means a fleshy fruit with a thin skin and one central stone containing the seed (like a cherry). The smooth skin has a green tint when young. The exocarp (outer skin) falls off and exposes the chalk-white mesocarp (middle layer). The fruit then looks like itsy-bitsy peeled oranges, with black lines (dried-out resin canals) between the segments. Drupes form in midsummer and hang in clusters. There is only one seed per drupe, which then later might be eaten by a little bird that proceeds to poop anywhere it pleases. The seed probably likes its new digs and, after the gummy seed coat sloughs off, it prepares to sprout in its little pile of nutritious manure.

RESIN

Resins are comprised of both nonvolatile (does not evaporate) and volatile components. The nonvolatile components make resin sticky, and they harden over time.

Resin has wide-ranging uses. Some resins are used for varnishes and adhesives. The resin of the Japanese lacquer tree, a close relative of poison oak and poison ivy (and even closer to poison sumac), was used by Stone Age peoples to glue spears and arrowheads onto shafts. Much later it was used as a hard membrane, covering everything from leather coats of armor to wooden chopsticks. The odor of incense is derived from the essential oil component of some resins. Herbalists make therapeutic use of certain essential oils. Amber is fossilized resin and is valuable for jewelry.

Jean Langenheim, author of *Plant Resins*, says resins "...apparently play no role in the primary or fundamental physiology of the plant, but are important in their defense against a variety of enemies such as insects, pathogens, mammalian herbivores." Resins do a good job of sealing a wound in the bark, which, like our skin, is a protective barrier.[12]

Urushiol, the oil that causes the rash, is part of the resin of poison oak, poison ivy and all other *Toxicodendrons*. Instead of occurring throughout the tissues, resin is contained in tiny, sometimes microscopic, interconnecting cavities—also called endogenous

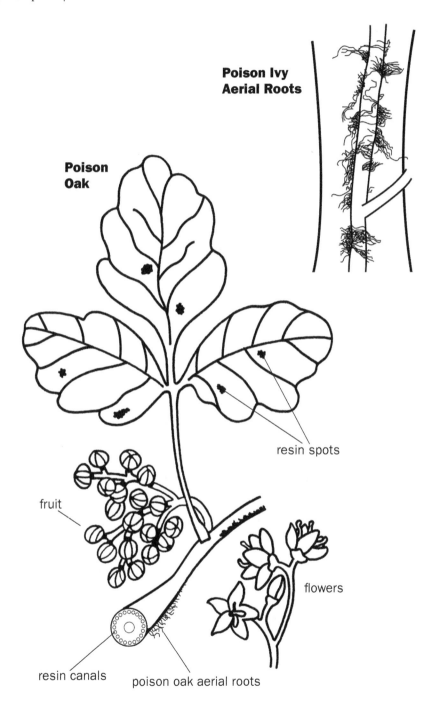

**Poison Ivy
Aerial Roots**

**Poison
Oak**

resin spots

fruit

flowers

resin canals   poison oak aerial roots

(having an internal origin) canals.[70] The system of canals is under pressure. If a canal is broken, resin flows to the surface and hardens to seal the wound. Compare this to getting a cut on your hand. As the blood dries, the wound is sealed.

A cross-section of a poison oak or poison ivy trunk exposes the resin canals, which lie in the phloem area, the inner living part of the bark. Each spring, new resin canals are formed and each canal is surrounded by special cells that synthesize and secrete the allergenic solution into the canals.[14] Using a magnifying glass, I cut a small leaf stem and observed the tiny duct ends, like numbers on a clock, dripping the clear allergenic resin. Later the cut end turned black upon being exposed to oxygen.

Resin canals develop in the roots, stems, leaves, flowers, branches and trunks. The parts of the plant lacking resin are the orange male flower anthers, hairs, wood cells (in the center of the stem or trunk), pollen and nectar.

Immature fruit (drupe) contains canals only while green. As the fruit matures, resin production slows down and edible fats begin building up. When the fruit is ripe, its resin canals have collapsed, creating a peeled orange effect when the outer epidermis falls off. The fruit is now nontoxic to humans, and a good source of fat for birds throughout the winter.

Before exposure to air, resin is clear. But sap leaking from a wound along with resin can turn the emerging liquid cloudy or milky.[70] After exposure to air, resin slowly darkens and hardens, becoming pitch-black. Sun degrades the dried resin, weakening the membrane and turning it a light gray over time.

Like the fangs of a baby rattlesnake, the emerging stem and leaves of a sprouted seed of poison oak or poison ivy come packaged with the stuff to do you in—their tiny resin canals are all in place.

Don't mistake resin with what is called "sap" (chiefly water with dissolved sugars and mineral salts). Sap moves throughout a plant using two separate types of cells: xylem and phloem. The xylem tissues consist of dead cells forming tubes in the center of the stem or trunk—the rings you observe on a tree stump. The outside layer is composed of new cells that will die in a year, creating a new ring. The dead xylem tissues move water and minerals upward from the roots, providing stiffness to the stems in the process. Phloem, the innermost layer of the bark, which is a living tissue, is involved in moving a mixture of water, carbohydrates and minerals throughout the plant. The word "sap" is not a scientific term and is often used indiscriminately.

Besides sap, some writers refer to the resin as "latex" (think rubber tree tapping). I quote from *Plant Resins*: "Latex is produced in vessels or special cells called laticifers, which are quite different from the internal secretory tissues (e.g., pockets, cavities or canals) in which most resin is produced."

All members of the family *Anacardiaceae* have resin channels. Some have allergenic chemicals in their resin that cross-sensitize with the allergenic oil in poison oak and poison ivy. So if you are allergic to poison ivy, you will probably be allergic to the resin in a mango skin and the oil between the two honeycombed layers of the cashew nut shell.

GROWING CONDITIONS

Poison oak and poison ivy both love sunshine, but also grow in moderate shade where the forest soil seems to be covered with ground-crawling and tree-climbing vines. The leaves in the shade are up to six inches long and seem flimsier and droopier than the two- or three-inch-long leaves of the shrubby thickets in sunny meadows. Plants in the shade seem healthy, but are always reaching for the sun—either lying over other plants toward a clearing or pathway, or climbing up tall trees.

To look its Sunday best, along with at least filtered sun, poison oak and poison ivy like relatively rich soil—a bit acidic, not too dry, not too moist. No arctic cold, desert conditions, or standing water, if you please. However, these tenacious plants do grow, even if small and scrawny, in more various conditions than most other shrubs—in shaded evergreen forests, woodlands, chaparral, coastal sage scrub, dry meadows and riparian zones (near moving water). Eastern poison oak (*T. pubescens*) and western poison ivy (*T. rydbergii*) prefer a leaner soil of sand and gravel.

Five thousand feet (occasionally six thousand) in altitude is the highest *Toxicodendrons* grow in the United States, although a hybrid of eastern poison ivy, *T. radicans ssp. divaricatum*, has been found enjoying the view at nine thousand feet in the Mexican mountains.

TRUNKS AND STEMS

An old gray-brown trunk of poison oak or poison ivy can look beat up, what with its moss and lichen, but new wood is very smooth with a pale-gray cast, sometimes with a tinge of orange. Stems usually grow long with short side branches appearing alternately (never directly) across from each other. Small triangular buds appear on the leafless branches during winter, opening in spring.

CLIMBING ABILITY

English ivy was the namesake for eastern poison ivy. Besides a vague similarity in leaves, they both climb using tiny roots, called aerial roots. These roots grow only aboveground along the trunk of the vine, and then tenaciously attach to a tree or fence post. Therefore, the plants have no need to twine for support; they can grow straight up. Eastern poison ivy has a great profusion of aerial roots and the vines often look like ratty old ropes. You need to look closely six to seven feet up the trunk to spot the tiny, sparse aerial roots of western poison oak. Both plants wedge their stems within crevices of the supporting plant or structure, seeming to become one with old outbuildings.

Growing up through the canopy of its host, peering into the sun, the trunk of a poison oak or poison ivy vine may look lifeless from below. Another of these plants might seem content to drape lazily over handy branches and enjoy the shade *below* the canopy. Often these stems poke out of a shrub at eye level into a pathway. I sometimes stop dead in my tracks when my **POISON OAK & POISON IVY**

AUTOMATIC SENSOR sends a warning to my brain that the stem about five inches from my nose should get another look.

These climbing vines do not take nutrients from their host tree, nor do they strangle them, although their foliage might hamper photosynthesis in a sun lover by creating shade. In 1991 B. L. Gartner experimented with western poison oak clones (all identical to the mother plant). He determined that "*T. diversilobum*, western poison oak, will grow as vines if given support, but as shrubs in the absence of support." Even an individual plant will develop both growth characteristics if some stems are supported and others are not. A single plant will become half vine and half shrub, with about seven structural differences between the two stem types (vines were less structurally stable, but grew faster, as one example). Gartner's conclusion was that growth variation in western poison oak is from "...environmental responses, not from different genetic races of origin."[14]

Eastern poison oak and western poison ivy, the lesser-known relatives to what are normally known as poison oak and poison ivy, both grow in shrub form only.

UNDERGROUND ROOTS

Poison oak and poison ivy have the same root system, called rhizomes. These fleshy roots, similar to iris rhizomes, are actually underground stems with roots growing down from them deeper into the soil. The rhizomes spread just under the surface of the soil. Soon a new plant sprouts, then another. In this way, a plant expands its circumference. I once observed a huge machine digging out tenacious thickets of poison oak at a cattle ranch in an attempt to reclaim the land for grazing, demonstrating the tenacious character of the plants.

FIRE

As summer wanes, the forests of our western states blaze with multiple fires. Western poison oak may be a beneficial soil stabilizer, but in fires it acts as a "ladder fuel," guiding fire up the trunk of the tree. The plants might burn to the ground, but undaunted, underground rhizomes later sprout like mad. The seeds also are pretty hardy. A burned-off hillside will soon be full of green leaflets defiantly fluttering in the breeze.[15]

WHAT THEY LOVE

These vegetative wanderers follow humans around. Our disturbed ground works well for them. They love sides of hiking trails, old buildings, rock walls, parks and orchards. My mailbox post is very popular. Someday I may find a letter addressed to *Toxicodendron diversilobum*.

THE FIVE ALLERGENIC RELATIVES
IN THE U.S.

WESTERN POISON OAK (also called Pacific poison oak)
Toxicodendron diversilobum

Formerly called: *Rhus lobatum*
                  Rhus diversilobum

Common name: Poison oak

Western poison oak grows from the Baja peninsula of Mexico up through California west of the Sierra Nevada Mountains, into Oregon and Washington west of the Cascade Mountains, and peters out in British Columbia.

A close relative, *Toxicodendron pubescens*, is called eastern poison oak. When folks on the West Coast say "poison oak," they mean western poison oak. When Easterners say "poison oak," they usually mean eastern poison oak, but most people and casual writers use the generic "poison oak" for both plants.

Western poison oak is hemmed in big-time. It would love to spread its wings and cover all of America. If it chanced to make it over the high mountains, the desert environment would stop it in its tracks.

Between 1825 and 1830, David Douglas was the first European to discover poison oak on the Columbia River. The meeting probably was memorable. He named the plant *Rhus lobatum*.[16] Although they share many traits, poison oak and poison ivy are separate species in the same genus, *Toxicodendron*. Two notable differences are that western poison oak sometimes produces more than the typical three leaflets per leaf, and the margins of the leaflets are always irregular. Some leaflets are highly lobed, while others are not. The tips of the leaflets are rounded rather than sharp. The surface may be flat, curled or even crumpled.[16]

In California, poison oak has the distinction of being the most prevalent wild shrub. It receives no laurels. Because of the proliferation of forest fires in the west, firefighters have a particularly hard time of it. The plants easily catch fire and the dangerous component of the plant, urushiol, becomes airborne in the soot and can cause serious reactions in the lungs and throat of anyone breathing in the smoke.

Western poison oak is adapted to a greater range of rainfall and temperature than most shrubs, and hangs out in many neighborhoods just to keep you on your guard. Step lightly in evergreen forests, woodlands, chaparral, sage and riparian zones (by rivers and creeks). If you stick to deserts, marshes and tops of high mountains, you still cannot relax—you now have to deal with cactus, soggy feet, and altitude sickness.

EASTERN POISON OAK (also called Atlantic poison oak) *Toxicodendron pubescens*

Sometimes called: *Toxicodendron toxicarium (poison bearing)*
T. diversilobum ssp. Pubescens

Formerly called: *Toxicodendron quercifolium (oak leaved)*

Toxicodendron compactum
Rhus quercifolium

Common names: poison oak, eastern poison oak, oakleaf poison ivy, oakleaf ivy, cow itch, poison tree.

Eastern poison oak apparently went unnoticed in botanical circles until 1762. In 1803 it was officially given its name.[17]

Articles written by easterners often say "poison oak" when they mean eastern poison oak. Westerners usually think all poison oak is on the west coast. I certainly did.

This short scrubby shrub is considered by some botanists to be a subspecies of western poison oak, but most consider it a separate species. Although *T. pubescens* is closely related to western poison oak, they don't have family get-togethers because they are rooted on opposite sides of the country.

Eastern poison oak doesn't even get the chance to hybridize with its neighbor poison ivy. Their ranges overlap but they grow in different types of soil. If they happen to live close to each other, the couples are romantically misaligned—their blossoms open on different time schedules. "I'm ready, sweetheart." "Well, I'm not."

Averaging about three feet, this plant is not a climber like western poison oak. The leaves and fruits are covered with short hairs, giving the plant a velvety look, hence the name "*pubescens*." The leaflets often have the classic oak-leaf shape of the eastern white oak, the shape we all know from Thanksgiving decorations.

The preferred soil is poor and sandy. *T. pubescens* grows among scrub oaks and in the Pine Barrens in the southeast states from New Jersey southward and westward to Texas.

EASTERN POISON IVY
Toxicodendron radicans

Formerly called: *Rhus toxicodendron*
　　　　　　　Toxicodendron
　　　　　　　Rhus radicans

Toxicodendron tripbyllu
Edera trifolia candensi
Frutex candensis epimediumfolio
Hedera trifolia candensis

Common names: Picry, climbing sumac, poor man's liquid amber,
               poison vine, mercury, markweed, poison creep,
               three-leafed ivy, gowitch, poison creep, poisonwood.

Poison ivy was named by Captain John Smith, around 1609 and
noted in a book he wrote in 1624. He wrongly suspected it was
related to English ivy. The plant first enthralled colonists with its
gorgeous fall hues. Later it showed its "true colors."[18]

The present name of "radicans" means rooting, referring to aerial
roots of a mature plant that cling to the host plant or post, causing
the vine to resemble an old frayed rope. These roots are a great way
to identify an eastern poison ivy vine.

There are around nine identified subspecies of *T. radicans*. So,
if you came across a poison ivy plant in the U.S. it would be one
of the following six: *ssp. divaricatum, eximium, negundo, pubens,
verrucosum,* or *radicans*. It is suspected that the colonists dealt
with ssp. radicans.

A variety of leaf shapes can be found on poison ivy plants, what
with the various subspecies and continual inbreeding. Poison ivy
leaflets differ from those of the poison oaks in that the tips are
more pointed. Eastern poison ivy inbreeds with another species
Toxicodendron rydbergii (called western poison ivy) where their
ranges overlap. Some botanists consider *T. rydbergii* to be a subspecies of eastern poison ivy.

Grouping eastern and western poison ivy together, they almost
cover the entire United States, except for the West Coast (western poison oak's domain), the Great Basin, Mohave Desert and tall
mountains.

When in dry meadows, eastern poison ivy can be a three-foot-tall
shrub, but in the damp shady forest, it can scamper to the top of a
tall tree.

WESTERN POISON IVY
Toxicodendron rydbergii

Formerly called: *Rhus rydbergii*

Common names: Non-climbing poison ivy, Canadian poison ivy,
                    northern poison ivy, Rydberg's poison ivy

Western poison ivy was once considered a subspecies of *T. radicans* (eastern poison ivy) and was later given a spot as a separate species. Some botanists still consider it a subspecies. It often hangs out with the more familiar eastern poison ivy on their border areas and hybridizes easily, making it hard for botanists to differentiate between the two, hence the frustration.

T. rydbergii might grow as a small shrub up to ten feet, but is usually no taller than three feet, with only a single stem. The plants may have a few short branches, or no branches at all, and are adapt at moving into mowed lawns. Left alone, the plants will form colonies to 20 ft. or more across. Watch out when wearing shorts.

T. rydbergii has the widest range in the U.S. of all the *Toxicodendrons*, and is the most northerly ranging of the species. It is prolific in the Rockies, likes to hang out high in the Appalachian Mountains, and tends to lie about on the beaches of Lake Erie. It manages to sneak into Oregon and Washington through the Columbia River Gorge and interbreed with poison oak. Besides enjoying the cool weather of southern Canada, western poison ivy meanders south of the Four Corners region down into Mexico. In these arid lands, the plant can be found along tiny creeks and under rock overhangs near springs.

Being such a short, upright shrub with no obvious twining tendencies, western poison ivy has no need for the grabbing abilities of eastern poison ivy's aerial roots, although it was once induced to produce aerial roots in a growth chamber.[19] The shapes of its leaflets vary, but usually are not lobed. Because each of the three leaflets are distinctly folded upwards at the midrib (like a butterfly), they are often described as spoon-shaped, which doesn't make sense to me because soup would run out either end. When pressed flat, they often are wider than anticipated.

Western poison ivy's leaves are usually smooth, but on some plants the full leaf or only the underside might be covered with fine hairs, giving the plant a downy look. The fruit tends to grow larger than the other *Toxicodendrons*, with a stiffer fruit stem.

Along with northerly climates, *T. rydbergii* enjoys sunny habitats like sandy or gravelly bottom lands, lakeshores and dunes.

POISON SUMAC

Toxicodendron vernix

Formally called: Rhus venenata, Rhus vernix

Common names: Poison weed, poison wood, poison tree, swamp
             sumac, varnish sumac, thunder wood, poison
             dogwood, poison ash, poison elder

Poison sumac is similar in appearance to some of the non-allergenic sumacs (winged, staghorn and smooth sumac). It was placed in the genus *Toxicodendron* from the genus *Rhus*. A number of other *Toxicodendrons* resemble sumacs in leaf form. There are five differences that put them all in with poison oak and poison ivy: 1. Presence of urushiol (the allergenic oil). 2. An absence of red glandular hairs on fruits and leaf stalks. 3. Pollen size (small). 4. Hanging flowers. 5. Color of fruit (cream or white).

Poison sumac loves the edges of marshes and bogs from Quebec to Florida, and west to a small area in east Texas. It especially likes the Great Lakes region. Away from moisture, it grows poorly. When ankle deep in water, don't get chummy with any sumac look-alikes you come upon. Real sumacs shun marshes.

Poison sumac is a small tree, sometimes just a shrub. It normally grows between fifteen and twenty feet, although it can grow to fifty feet if conditions are right. It is fast-growing, but short-lived.

Leaves are composed of a stem with four or more sets of leaflets. One leaflet at the tip (terminal leaflet) completes the leaf. Each leaflet is about three to four inches long, one to two inches wide, and resembles the shape of a rabbit ear. Leaflet edges are smooth. They start out orange when young, later turning dark green with lighter green on the undersides. The midrib from which the leaflets grow is always red. The complete leaf consisting of the leaflets may reach fifteen or more inches in length. The leaves turn red, orange and yellow in the fall. Poison sumac leaves do not resemble those of poison oak and poison ivy, but the fruit and flowers do.

The fruit hang in large drooping clusters. Like poison oak and poison ivy, only the female plants bear fruit.

The trunk can be from one to five inches in diameter, and the bark is a pale gray. The wood is light and brittle and contains much pith (soft or spongy tissue). Tips of young shoots are usually an attractive red.

For a brief period in 1756 there was a flurry of excitement in botanical quarters. It was argued that the Japanese lacquer tree *Toxicodendron vernicifluum* (source of a high-quality allergenic resin used for the lacquer products of China, Japan and Korea) and poison sumac were one and the same. Others argued that the botanical descriptions didn't match. In 1809, *The Philosophical Transactions of the Royal Society of London* brought up the subject, which was again put on the back burner.[20] It is now known that poison sumac and the Japanese lacquer tree split off from a common ancestor about seven and a half million years ago.[16]

In 1814, Jacob Bigelow, author of *American Medical Botany*, had reason to believe the "twin" theory and set out to prove that poison sumac was no slacker in its ability to produce high quality lacquer.

Probably wearing waders, Dr Bigelow, with an assistant (who later paid dearly for the days outing among the highly allergenic shrubs), took to the marshes. Tapping sumac trees, they collected a copious amount of resin. Back in his lab, he began painting his bounty on wood, glass, tinned iron, paper and cloth. Since Dr Bigelow was unaware that urushiol needs moisture to "dry," the painted objects sat for two months in an arid environment and remained tacky. Undaunted, the doctor boiled the resin, allowing most of the moisture to evaporate, and then spread the goopy mess on his test objects. The resin eventually dried, leaving a brilliant, glossy, jet-black surface, so durable and elastic that it seemed "calculated to answer the purposes of both paint and varnish." He did note a "very distressing, cutaneous disease."

After this dramatic beginning, his last comment was "The introduction of the juice into the arts will not perhaps take place during the present high price of labor, and the general prejudice which exists against the shrub." But, he did leave us with the hope that one day such a valuable resource will not be neglected. Fat chance.[21]

WHICH PLANT CAUSES THE WORST RASH

Most folks are unlikely to run into poison sumac—unless marsh slogging becomes a popular extreme sport. I've noticed a number of claims by serious researchers that the allergenic oil of poison sumac has a stronger allergic potential than that of poison oak and poison ivy. As far back as 1817, Jacob Bigelow wrote, "The *Rhus vernix* is the most formidable of this tribe." In 1887 James Clark White noted its potency. He said, "I have observed that persons who have always handled poison ivy with impunity became more susceptible to its influence after having been poisoned by the more virulent poison sumac."[22] As late as 1991, botanist Edward Frankel wrote, "To some botanists and all its victims, poison sumac is our most poisonous plant."[16]

Westerners have a morbid theory that poison oak has a stronger allergenic potential than "wimpy" poison ivy, whose supporters vehemently disagree with that assessment.

Dedicated poison oak researcher Albert Kligman took the bull by the horns in 1957. He applied bruised fresh leaves of poison oak, ivy and sumac to the backs of heroic individuals who were moderately sensitive. **All rashes were equal**. Now that's settled. End of subject.[23]

References

1. USDA. 2011 "Classification for Kingdom Plantae Down to Species Toxicodendron diversilobum." www.plants.usda.gov.

2. Pell, Susan K. 2009. "Anacardiaceae Cashew Family." Tree of Life Project. www.tolweb.org.

3. Mitchell, John, and Arthur Rock. 1979. *Botanical Dermatology: Plants Injurious to the Skin.* Greenslash Ltd., Canada.

4. Nie, Ze-Long, et al. 2009. "Phylogenetic Analysis of Toxicodendron: Anacardiaceas and Its Biogeographic Implications on the Evolution of North Temperate and Tropical Intercontinental Disjunctions." *Journal of Systematics and Evolution* 47(5):416-430.

5. Crosby, Donald G. 2004. *The Poisoned Weed.* Oxford University Press, NY.

6. Angiosperm Phylogeny Group. 2009. en.wikipedia.org.

7. Senchina, David S. 2008. "Fungal and Animal Associates of Toxicodendron spp. Anacardiaceae) in North America." *Perspectives in Plant Ecology, Evolution and Systematics* 10:197-216.

8. Gillis, William T. 1975. "Poison Ivy and Its Ken." Arnoldia 35(2).

9. Beebe, Curt. 2010. Web site devoted to poison oak information. www.curtbeebe.com.

10. Winterringer, Glen S. 1963. *Poison-Ivy and Poison-Sumac: Their Growth Habits and Variations.* Illinois State Museum. Story of Illinois Series No. 13.

11. Senchina, David S., and Keith S. Summerville. 2007. "Great Diversity of Insect Floral Associates May Partially Explain Ecological Success of Poison Ivy." *The Great Lakes Entomologist* 40(3&4):120-128.

12. Langenheim, Jean H. 2003. *Plant Resins: Chemistry, Evolution, Ecology, and Ethnobotany.* Timber Press, Portland, OR.

13. "Poison Ivy." 1926. Field Museum of Natural History Leaflet 12. Dept. of Botany,Chicago.

14. Gardner, B.L. 1991. "Is the Climbing Habit of Poison Oak Ecotypic?" *Functional Ecology* 5(5):696-704.

15. Howard, June T. n.d. *"Index of Species Information."* Fire Effects Information System, US Dept. of Agriculture, Forest Service, Rocky Mountain Research Station.

16. Frankel, Edward. 1991. *Poison Ivy, Poison Oak, Poison Sumac and Their Relatives.* Boxwood Press, CA.

17. McNair, James B. 1925. *The Taxonomy of Poison Ivy.* Field Museum of Natural History, Chicago.

18. "Poisonous Plants Have Painful Bite." 1998. Post Tribune. Gary, IN.

19. Gillis, William T. 1971. "The Systematics and Ecology of Poison Ivy and the Poison Oaks. (*Toxicodendron Anacardiaceae*)." Rhodora, vol. 73.

20. Ellis, John. 1809. *The Philosophical Transactions of the Royal Society of London*, vol. 11.

21. Bigelow, Jacob. 1817. *American Medical Botany.* Cummings and Hilliard, Boston.

22. White, James Clark. 1887. *Dermatitis Venenata*.

23. Kligman, Albert M. 1957. "Poison Ivy (Rhus) Dermatitis: An Experimental Study." Archives of Dermatology 77(2):149-180.

TRACINGS FROM COLLECTED LEAVES

Western Poison Oak
Toxicodendron diversilobum

Eastern Poison Oak
Toxicodendron pubescens

Eastern Poison Ivy
Toxicodendron radicans

 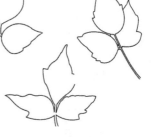

Western Poison Ivy
Toxicodendron rydbergii

MAPS OF POISON OAK, IVY, & SUMAC IN NORTH AMERICA
(Edges of ranges are not as distinct as maps indicate)

Western Poison Oak
Toxicodendron diversiloba

Specimens were collected from
these states: CA, OR, WA

Eastern Poison Ivy
Toxicodendron radicans

Specimens were collected from
these states: AL, AR, AZ, CT, DC,
DE, GL, GA, IA, IL, IN, KS, KY, LA,
MA, MD, ME, MI, MN, MO, MS, NC,
NE, NH, NJ, NY, OH, OK, PA, RI,
SC, SD, TN, TX, VA, VT, WI, WV

Eastern Poison Oak
Toxicodendron pubescens

Specimens were collected from
these states: AL, AR, DC, DE, FL,
GA, IL, KS, LA, MD, MO, MS, NC,
NJ, OK, SC, TN, TX, VA, WV

Western Poison Ivy
Toxicodendron rydbergii

Specimens were collected from
these states: AR, ID, IL, IN, IA KS,
ME, MA, MI, NM, MT, NE, NH, NM,
NC, ND, OK, OR, PA, SD, TX,
UT, VT, WA, WV, WI, WY

Poison Sumac
Toxicodendron vernix

Specimens were collected from
these states: AL, CT, DC, DE, FL,
GA, IL, IN, KY, LA, MA, MD, ME, MI,
MN, MS, NC, NH, NJ, NY, OH, PA,
RI, SC, TN, TX, VA

See these photos in color at **www.poisonoakandpoisonivy.com**

Leaflets of western poison ivy usually fold up from the midrib like wings of a butterfly. It often interbreeds with eastern poison ivy.

(Photo by Daniel Boelman)

Western poison oak easily climbs a redwood tree. Allergenic resin leaking from a bark wound soon hardens and turns pitch black.

(Photo by author)

Poison Sumac. Looking like a sumac, this plant is actually closely related to poison oak and poison ivy.

(Ted Bodner@USDA-NRCS Plants Database/ James H. Miller and Karl V. Miller. 2005 *Forest Plants of the Southeast and Their Wildlife Uses.* University of Georgia Press. Athens)

See these photos in color at **www.poisonoakandpoisonivy.com**

Young western poison oak
leaves emerge red-bronze
and slowly turn green.
(Photo by author)

This beautiful eastern poison ivy vine
is obviously loved and pruned as it
hugs a garden shed.
(Photo by Judy Feller)

Western poison oak with flowers.
Notice the scalloped leaflets
have no sharp points.
(Photo by author)

These western poison oak branches, gracefully hanging over a path,
are a trap for the unwary walker.
(Photo by author)

See these photos in color at **www.poisonoakandpoisonivy.com**

The leaflets of eastern poison ivy have sharper points than those of western and eastern poison oaks. This is a young vine with few aerial roots.

(Photo by John Paine)

Some mature eastern poison ivy vines have such a thick covering of aerial roots, they look like rotten old ropes.

(Photo by Judy Feller)

Eastern poison oak does not grow as a vine. The leaflets are often covered with tiny hairs.

(Used by permission from www.walterreeves.com)

See these photos in color at **www.poisonoakandpoisonivy.com**

Two mature leaves of western poison oak from one plant on the author's acreage. (Tsk, tsk—the hand should be wearing a glove.)
(Photo by author)

Western poison oak is snuggling into cracks in the bark of the ponderosa pine as it grows upward. Notice the pine's light colored resin dripping down—quite different from the thinner pitch-black resin of poison oak and poison ivy.
(Photo by author)

Western poison oak, when climbing, has pitifully small aerial roots compared with those of eastern poison ivy.
(Photo by author)

Note white color, and lines resembling orange segments. The fruit is drying out as summer progresses.
(Photo by author)

Out for a stroll.

Chapter 3

RELATIVES AROUND THE WORLD

JAPANESE LACQUER TREE
Toxicodendron vernicifluum

Formally called: *Rhus vernicifluum.*

Common names: Urushi tree, Rhus varnish tree, Japanese varnish
tree, Japanese sumac, oriental lacquer tree,
Chinese lacquer tree.

The Japanese lacquer tree is fabulous. If not for this tree, few of
us would know how amazing urushiol could be. Yes, that very same
stuff in poison oak and poison ivy that kept you up for five nights
scratching. Each member of the genus *Toxicodendron* has slightly
different urushiol chemistry and *vernicifluum* has the best—in a
useful way.

It is not common knowledge in the U.S. that in Japan, China and
Korea, these trees are tapped for the valuable resin that contains 60
to 75 percent urushiol. In fact, the tree is a close relative to poison
sumac, being taller, but with similar leaves. The Japanese lacquer
tree resin, called urushi, is believed to have been used by peoples
of the Stone Age as an adhesive for spears and arrows. In China,
urushi has been collected for more than seven thousand years.[1] The
Japanese were possibly the first to paint with urushi nine thousand
years ago, but the Chinese perfected and kept secret a special technique for processing and applying the lacquer. The Japanese finally

obtained the secret process more than two thousand years ago, about the time the Koreans began working with lacquer.[2] Lacquerware was introduced to Europe in the seventeenth century. Of the three countries, China leads the world in production and export.[3]

The beautiful kitchenware (bowls and utensils), furniture, musical instruments and exquisite artwork—distinctive for bright colors and the deep, smooth shine—are not delicate. The lacquer creates a deceptively tough membrane. It has an amazing resistance to corrosion, abrasion, dampness, heat, salt, mildew, acid and alkalinity. It has been painted on wood, pottery, bone, baskets, fabric, leather, hardened rubber and metal, and is used by industrial companies to coat pipes and wiring, and as an adhesive, among other industrial uses. Lacquer has one Achilles heel: it breaks down in ultraviolet light (the sun). These days, chemical additives solve this problem for industrial uses.[1]

While in leaf, fifteen- to twenty-foot trees are tapped for the resin by scoring the bark and hanging a container beneath. Japan, China and Korea each have their own technique for tapping and processing the thick liquid. An acquaintance visited a Japanese lacquer tree plantation and told me she observed a fellow who seemed to be responsible for a certain number of trees. He carefully monitored them, wielding a spatula-like tool. As urushi slowly oozed from the tree, he guided it into the hanging can below. Urushi is considered "alive," and in a way, it is. You could consider it the lifeblood of the tree, for when the tree is wounded (tapped), it flows out. Over-tapping will kill the tree, and in some places, it is done on purpose to obtain more resin.[4]

Fresh from the tree, the resin comes diluted with 25 to 65 percent water (usually called sap). Sap contains minerals and sugars from the nutritional system of the tree, which can turn the resin cloudy as the sap flows out along with the resin when the bark is scored. Urushi begins to harden when exposed to oxygen so it is quickly filtered and sealed in an airtight container. Grading urushi depends on many factors: species of *vernicifluum*, age of tree, part of country grown, soil type, season collected, whether it experienced heat, and even the smell.[3]

The "raw" urushi is gently heated to 104°F in an open vat. It is stirred for approximately four hours, while 96 to 98 percent of the water evaporates, until it is smooth and dark brown. Other details are kept secret, and differ between countries and manufacturers. We do know that adding iron oxides creates colors.[2, 5]

The process of making a piece of artwork using urushi can take weeks, months, or with large, elaborate pieces, years to complete. Each layer is dried, sanded and sometimes decorated or etched before the next layer is applied.[6]

Most paints dry through evaporation of a solvent or water, but urushi (including the urushiol of poison oak and poison ivy) doesn't dry by the usual means. The piece is placed in a warm cabinet or room with high humidity. This seems counterproductive, but the warmth and moisture activates an enzyme, *laccase*, that aids in pulling oxygen from the water vapor (remember, water is comprised of oxygen and hydrogen). This causes urushiol to harden from oxidation and it polymerizes, creating a protective covering. In other words, a dry environment *slows* "drying," and a moist environment *hastens* "drying," diminishing the allergenic properties, especially when combined with heat. An added twist is that the slower the drying, the stronger the lacquer membrane.[7] There should be around 3 percent moisture left in the finished product,[2] "which is soft and natural and never becomes brittle as plastics do."[4]

A 1992 study determined that heat is extremely important to complete polymerization because even a hardened membrane can be allergenic—as their test pieces showed. Volunteers were patch-tested by heat-treated and nonheat-treated lacquer. The reactions were stronger from the nonheated pieces. It seems that if heat is *insufficient* during the process, it can take six to ten years for the piece to become nonallergenic on its own, without heat *and* moisture. The researchers wrote, "When the temperature rises 10°C, the velocity of the chemical reaction doubles, thus the reaction at 20°C (68°F) for ten years is equivalent to the reaction at 150°C (302°F) for 11 hours."[7]

You would think that because of close contact to the many

urushi-lacquered products in China, Japan and Korea, most everyone in those countries develops a complete tolerance from an early age. But not so—Japanese clinics record a brisk business in treating contact dermatitis.

The chemistry of urushiol in poison oak and poison ivy is slightly different from the urushiol of the Japanese lacquer tree. For example, poison oak and poison ivy resins don't cure well enough for lacquer production, specifically because of the high diene content—an unsaturated hydrocarbon containing two double bonds between carbon atoms, as opposed to the three double bonds (high triene content) of the Japanese lacquer tree.[2] I thought I would let you know in case you were considering tapping a poison oak or poison ivy vine to paint a wooden bowl.

I spent an evening chatting with an artist who studied the art of lacquer painting in Japan. She said urushi is considered a spiritual, emotional medium. "Your body bonds with it." When her teacher visited San Francisco, he literally embraced poison oak plants, and excitedly gathered seeds to grow in Japan. Far from being careful around urushi, he paints with his hands instead of brushes.[4]

You may need to re-read this chapter to comprehend why the garden tools you used to dig up poison ivy might still be allergenic next year if stored in a cool, dry shed.

OTHER RELATIVES

Toxicodendron striatum

Common name: Manzanillo.

This shrub or small tree, with eleven to fifteen leaflets per leaf stem, grows from South Mexico to Bolivia. It is very common in parts of Guatemala and Costa Rica and is highly feared. Luckily, it is easily recognized.

Toxicodendron succedaneum

Common name: Japanese wax tree.

Growing up to twenty-five feet tall, this large shrub or tree resembles a sumac and is a popular garden plant in Japan. It also grows in India, Thailand, Brazil and Australia. A wax (sumac wax) is extracted from the fruit for use in varnishes, polishes, ointments, candles and other products.

Toxicodendron borneense

Growing in the tropical forests of Borneo, this plant is very rare and is an unusual example of the species, having three-inch by six-inch single leaves as opposed to the multiple leaflets on one leaf stem of other toxicodendrons.

Toxicodendron nodosum

This plant has five to seven leaflets per leaf stem and grows as a vine to about fifty feet in Indonesia and Malaysia.

Toxicodendron trichocarpum

This large shrub or small tree is very similar to the Japanese lacquer tree and grows in China, Japan and Korea.

Toxicodendron wallichii: China.

Toxicodendron fulvum: China, Thailand.

Toxicodendron delarayi: China.

Toxicodendron grandaflorum: China.

Toxicodendron griffithii: China

Toxicodendron hookerti: China, India

Toxicodendron yunnanense: China

Toxicodendron sylvestre: China, Japan, Korea and Taiwan.

References

1. Stutler, Russ. n.d. "A Little More Information on Urushi." www.pentrace.net/east/ wajima/jurushi.html.

2. Vogl, Otto. 2000. "Oriental Lacquer, Poison Ivy, and Drying Oils." *Journal of Polymer Science* 38(24):4327-4335.

3. Webb, Marianne. 2000. *Lacquer: Technology and Conservation.* Butterworth-Heinemann.

4. Higby, Sha Sha. 2010. Sculptor. Telephone interview. www.shashahigby.com.

5. Mills, John S., and Raymond White. 1987. *The Organic Chemistry of Museum Objects.* Butterworth-Heinemann.

6. "Lacquer." n.d. Bishop Museum, Hawaii.

7. Kawai, K., M. Nakagawa, T. Milyakoshi, K. Miyashita, and T. Asami. 1992. "Heat Treatment of Japanese Lacquerware Renders It Hypoallergenic." *Contact Dermatitis* 27(4):244-249.

Poison sumac. *Toxicodendron vernix.*

(Closely related to Japanese Lacquer Tree *Toxicodendron vernicifluum)*

Illustration from USDA-NRCS PLANTS Database

Oh, we don't do fire anymore...

Chapter 4

PLANTS THAT CROSS SENSITIZE with POISON OAK and POISON IVY

MANGO

Mangifera indica
Family: *Anacardiaceae*

Mango is my favorite fruit—the huge orange and red, super-juicy varieties. One of my greatest challenges is successfully gauging what seems to be the twenty minutes or so a ripening globe is at its peak of perfection.

Mango is a tree that cross-reacts with poison oak, poison ivy, cashew and ginkgo. If you are allergic to one, you are probably allergic to the others.[1, 2] Surprisingly, most folks never realize that by eating a mango, they are at risk of developing an itchy rash.

The peel of the fruit contains a high concentration of the branching multilayered network of resin ducts containing 5-heptadecenylresorcinol. Resorcinol is a crystalline phenol in various resins. Besides being allergenic, it is caustic enough to leave burn-like scars when the transparent yellowish-tan resin drips from a fresh stem cut.[3, 4]

The allergenic compound does not form in the pulp of the fruit, but can bleed at least a quarter of an inch from the peel into the pulp.[5]

Anyone *highly* allergic to poison oak and poison ivy should stay away from all mango products.

Studies have shown that commercial processing of mango pulp (heating, pureeing, freezing, juicing, etc.) does not destroy the allergenic capabilities.[6, 7, 8]

Dale Erickson, a mango grower in Florida, says his new workers usually develop allergic reactions, but most become fairly tolerant over time. I found it interesting that he has never noticed his family or employees develop rashes with blisters. The norm is an itchy red rash that bothers workers a lot "only when it moves below the belt," Dale said.[9]

A study in 1966 indicated ***mango allergenic chemicals are not as potent a sensitizer as those of poison oak and poison ivy,*** at least when applied to the skin of guinea pigs. It required a very high concentration to achieve a reaction.[10] Tell that to author Tom Ogren and he will probably snort. Out of six siblings, four of them are highly allergic to mango. His lips and nose swell up to "Mr. Potato Head" proportions.[11] I also have two case reports of anaphylactic-like shock reactions following ingestion of mango pulp.[12, 13]

Locals in mango-growing areas are typically pretty tolerant to the mango resin, whereas visitors often get rashes. A study that compared mango pickers in Israel with a group of American students who all were allergic to poison oak noted that each student suffered itchy dermatitis, whereas the local pickers were not affected.[14] This is an example of why a number of researchers have suspected what Kenneth Lampe wrote in 1986: ***"The eating of mango in infancy and continuously thereafter may result in oral desensitization."***[15]

Mango trees are cultivated throughout the tropics, but there are also mango plantations in Florida and southern California, so we are seeing more mangos in supermarkets these days. Although the allergenic oil in the skin of the fruit apparently is not as strong as poison oak and poison ivy oil, if you develop an unexplained rash around your mouth and chin after eating a mango, you'll know why.

CASHEW
Anacardium occidentale
Family: *Anacardiaceae*

In the 1900s, a fellow bought a container of cashew butter, recently ground by the storeowners from raw cashew nuts. He loved it and scooped up the tasty treat with his fingers. It took awhile to figure out why he developed a rash on his hand and his anus. He was allergic to an oil in cashews that cross-reacts with poison oak and poison ivy. If you are allergic to one, you are allergic to the other.

Cashew trees grow only in the tropics; even the climate in Florida is too darned chilly for their liking. The cashews we in the U.S. purchase already have been shelled and heated, even the ones labeled "raw." Why heat the nuts? To neutralize any allergenic resin in the honeycomb structure of the cashew shell might have migrated to the nut. This resin contains two allergenic oils, anacardiol and cardol, that cross-react with poison oak and poison ivy.

Somehow, the store obtained cashews that had not undergone the heating process. They were truly raw. The customer ate a large amount of the cashew butter, resulting in a rash on his hand. His mucus membranes protected his mouth and digestive system, but the allergenic chemicals came out the back door potent as ever and still able to cause a rash in an extremely inconvenient spot.[16]

Urushiol from poison oak and poison ivy is not damaged by heat. If the oil were heated in a pan, it would not vaporize or change its toxicity (not that you would want to use urushiol to pop your popcorn). The oil of the cashew *shell*, however, can be chemically changed by heat and will no longer cause an allergic reaction. But the fumes from the process can be dangerous and can cause an allergic reaction on skin and in the lungs of anyone leaning over the pot.

The oil of the cashew nut itself (called cashew oil) is considered an excellent vegetable oil. It is very soothing when used in skin creams; obviously, it does not contain allergenic chemicals. The oil from the inside of the double shell, though, is a different matter; it is highly allergenic. It is called cashew nut shell liquid (CNSL) and has many industrial uses such as friction linings (car brakes, e.g.), paints, laminating and resins among others. Many workers in these factories do develop allergic reactions from contact with the CNSL, but studies have shown that with time, most become desensitized enough to continue working the same jobs.[17, 18]

GINKGO
Ginkgo Biloba
Family: *Ginkgoaceae*

Common name: Maidenhair tree

Along a good many American city streets, folks stroll under beautiful maidenhair trees with fan-shaped leaves. Of the female and male trees, females produce fruit that drops to the ground and later becomes a stinky mess. Thankfully, only male trees are sold in nurseries these days.

Ginkgo shares chemicals with poison oak, poison ivy, mango and cashew. Immunological cross-reactivity is possible. If you are already allergic to any of the others, you are probably allergic to ginkgo's ginkgolic acid, which is found throughout the stems, flowers and leaves, and is especially abundant in the pulp of the foul-smelling fruit. The seed, however, is free of allergens and is a culinary delight in the East.[19, 20] In 2002 it was discovered that there is a small amount of urushiol (the allergenic oil in poison oak and poison ivy) in ginkgo tree resin.[19]

I'm slightly allergic to poison oak but I had no reaction to ginkgo tree resin smeared on my forearm and left for the day. Without the fruit, the trees are not much of an allergenic threat, although ginkgo supplements will be contaminated with the allergenic chemicals unless they are removed during processing. Europe has standards for this, but the U.S. has standards only for flavonoids and triperpenes.[21]

FOUR MORE SUSPECTS

These four plants are *suspected* of cross-reacting with poison oak and poison ivy

BRAZILIAN PEPPER TREE
Schinus terebinthifolius
Family: *Anacardiaceae*

Common names in Florida: Florida holly, Florida poison tree, hog gum, Christmas berry.

This shrub is native to Brazil and was introduced into Cuba, Puerto Rico, Mexico, California and Florida as an ornamental. It is now a huge pest in the central and southern parts of Florida. It is a tall shrub with arching branches. The leaf stem has a narrow wing between each of the three to eleven leaflets. When the leaves are crushed, there is a pronounced peppery-turpentine odor.

An allergenic phenol, also present in the allergenic cashew nut shell oil, is implicated in the sensitizing action. I read in *Dermatologic Botany* that although dermatologists in Florida consider there is a cross-reaction with poison ivy, this theory is unproven.[22]

I have read that the Brazilian pepper tree is the most common cause of allergic contact dermatitis in southern Florida. A friend who is a plant research geneticist is often exposed to pepper trees. He is moderately allergic to poison ivy, but has never had a reaction from these trees, nor has he heard of anyone else reacting. He does react strongly to poisonwood trees. On the other hand, plant allergy specialist and author Tom Ogren says that (especially when pruning) an allergic skin reaction to these trees is fairly common.[11]

POISONWOOD TREE
Metopium toxiferum
Family: *Anacardiaceae*

Common names: Florida poison tree, hog gum.

The poisonwood tree is fairly common in south Florida and the Keys. It also grows in Cuba, Haiti and Puerto Rico as a shrub or tree and has five to seven leaflets per leaf stem. The flaking bark exposes the orange color beneath. The resin contains C-15 catechols similar to those in poison oak and poison ivy.

PROTEA
Grevillea banksii
Family: *Proteaceae*

Grevillea contain a pentadecylresorcinol that may cross-react with poison oak and poison ivy, but is a weaker sensitizer. *Grevillea banksii* is a significant cause of allergic contact dermatitis in Hawaii.

INDIAN MARKING TREE
Semecarpus anacardium
Common names: Indian marking tree, Dhobi tree.

Growing in Southeast Asia, Pacific islands, and Australia, this tree is best known for the resin that Indian laundry workers used as an ink to mark customers' laundry. The tree was noticed by the West when American soldiers in the 1940s developed rashes when wearing freshly laundered garments. Repeated washing had little effect on the allergenic potency. I have numerous articles that repeat this story as if this quaint laundry identification technique is ongoing, but since the invention of indelible pens, I suspect the job of collecting and cooking the allergenic resin from the dhobi nut has faded from lack of enthusiasm.

In 2002, two of these attractive trees were removed from the grounds of the University of Hawaii after a raft of mysterious student rashes. The botany department showed their identification prowess and closed the case.

References

1. Knight, T.E., W.L. Epstein, and A.K. Prasad. 1996. "Resorcinols and Catechols: A Clinical Study of Cross Sensitivity." *Amer. J. of Contact Dermatitis* 7(3):138-145.

2. Oka, K., F. Saito, T. Yasuhara, and A. Sugimoto. 2004. "A Study of Cross-Reactions between Mango Contact Allergens and Urushiol." *Contact Dermatitis* 51:292-296.

3 "Mango Botany and Taxonomy." 2009. www.horticultureworld.net.

4. Oka, K., F. Saito, T. Yasuhara, and A. Sugimoto. 2004. "A Study of Cross Reactions between Mango Contact Allergens and Urushiol." *Contact Dermatitis* 51:292-296.

5. Weinstein, Sari. 2004. "Allergic Contact Dermatitis to Mango Flesh." *International Journal of Dermatology* 43:195-196.

6. Thoo, Caroline, and Susi Freeman. 2008. "Hypersensitivity Reaction to the Ingestion of Mango Flesh." Skin and Cancer Foundation, Australia.

7. Knodlert, Matthias, Katharina Reisenhauert, Andreas Schieber, and Reinhold Carlet. 2009. "Quantitative Determination of Allergenic 5-Alk(en)ylresorcinols in Mango (Mangifera indica L.) Skin, Pulp, and Fruit Products by High-Performance Liquid Chromatography." *J. Agric. Food Chem.* 57:3639-3644.

8. Dube, Mark, Katy Zunker, Sybille Neidhart, Reinhold Carle, Hans Steinhart, and Angelika Paschke. 2004. "Effect of Technological Processing on the Allergenicity of Mangos (Mangifera indica L.)." *J. Agric. Food Chem.* 52:3938-3945.

9. Erickson, Dale. 2010. Mango grower. Phone interview. www.ericksonfarm.com.

10. Baer, Harold. 1986. "Chemistry and Immunochemistry of Poisonous *Anacardiaceae*." *Clinics in Dermatology* 4(2):152-159.

11. Ogren, Thomas Leo. 2011. Author of *Allergy-Free Gardening*. E-mail correspondence.

12. Rubin, James M., Shapiro, Jerome, Muehlbauer, Peter, and Max Grolnick. 1965. "Shock Reaction Following Ingestion of Mango." JAMA. 193(5); 147-148.

13. Hedge, V.L., and Y.P. Venkatesh. 2007 "Anaphylaxis Following Ingestion of Mango Fruit." *J. Investig. Allersol. Clin. Immunol* 17(5):341-344.

14. Hershko, K., I. Weinberg, and A. Ingber. 2005. "Exploring the Mango-Poison Ivy Connection: The Riddle of Discriminative Plant Dermatitis." *Contact Dermatitis* 52(1):3-5.

15. Lampe, Kenneth D. 1986. *"Dermatitis-Producing Anacardiaceae of the Carribbean Area."* Cl. in Derm. 4(2):179-182.

16. Rosen, Ted, and Dawn B. Fordroe. 1994. "Cashew Nut Dermatitis." *Southern Medical Journal* 87(4).

17. Kligman, Albert M. 1958. "Cashew Nut Shell Oil for Hyposensitization against Rhus Dermatitis." *AMA Arch Derm* 78(3).

18. Reginella, Ruthane F., James C. Fairfield, and James G. Marks, Jr. 1989. "Hyposensitization to Poison Ivy after Working in a Cashew Nut Shell Oil Processing Factory." *Contact Dermatitis* 20(4):274-279.

19. Schotz, Karl. 2004. "Quantification of Allergenic Urushiols in Extracts of Ginkgo Biloba Leaves, in Simple One-Step Extracts and Refined Manufactured Material." *Phytochem Anal* 15(1):1-8.

20. Cartayrade, A., G. Bourgeois, J.P. Balz, and J.P. Carde. 1990. "The Secretory Apparatus of Gingko Biloba: Structure, Differentiation and Analysis of the Secretory Product." *Trees: Structure and Function* 4(4):171-178.

21. "If You Take Ginkgo Extract, Watch Out for Ginkgolic Acid." 2008. www.smartpublications.com.

22. Avalos, Javier, and Howard I. Maibach, eds. 2000. *Dermatologic Botany.* CRC Press, NY.

Perfected my special cure for poison
oak, flat feet, and rigor mortis.

Chapter 5

HISTORY

DNA CLUES TO EVOLUTION

Most of us don't care a whit where poison oak and poison ivy first developed, how their seeds moved around the world on animal fur and in birds intestines—or when they split from the mother plant and developed separate traits. Some researchers, though, carefully search for the answers. Although fossil clues were studied in the past, these days, genes and complicated technology yield more answers.

Multiple migrations are thought to have occurred between Asia and North America across the Bering land bridge, between what is now Russia and Alaska. The more tropical plants possibly moved across the Atlantic Ocean on land called the North Atlantic land bridge.[1]

One of the questions is: in which direction was the migration—from Asia to the new world, or the other way around? Susan Pell, a specialist in the genus (*Toxicodendron*) of poison oak, poison ivy and poison sumac, said the answer "...is not known definitively."[2] I have seen theories for both ways.

The most recent genetic analysis of the genus was in 2009.[1] Researcher Jun Wen, who worked on the study, says research on DNA strongly supports the *Toxicodendron* genus as having evolved as a distinct group.[3] There were two lineages that moved between eastern Asia and North America. One lineage consisted of poison oak and poison ivy species. The other lineage included poison sumac and the Japanese lacquer tree from China, Japan and Korea, plus various other species that resemble sumacs.[1]

COLONISTS AND POISON IVY—FACE-TO-FACE

Colonists first encountered poison ivy after landing in America, and the introductions were not pleasant. Captain John Smith (of Pocahontas fame, who would have been astounded had he known his destiny to end up as a cartoon character in a Disney movie) is considered to be the first, pen in hand in 1624, to discuss the "poisoned weed."[4]

Surprisingly, Smith was rather gentle in his description of this powerful plant and even went so far as to say, "It hath got it selfe an ill name, although questionless of no ill nature."[4] This was very gracious on his part. I collected a few quotes from writers throughout the years railing at what seems to them to be an evil, conscious nature of the plant:

> "Why are the tissues and fluids of three species of rhus...capable of inflicting an injury upon the only being for whom they are supposed to have been created...We may believe that the poison plants are the criminal class, because vegetable nature is sometimes evil." (James Clark White, *Dermatitis Venenata* 1887).

> "Poison ivy flourishes like the wicked." (*Country Life in America*, 1908)

> "Snake of the weeds. Whether it stands or crawls it is the same old Satan and should be designated as such." (Edwin Rollin Spencer, *All About Weeds*, 1940)

> "Poison ivy is your enemy." (Kim Painter, *USA Today*, 2006)

It seems the plants had evil feelings only for "palefaces," because Native Americans, although respecting the potential for serious side effects, were using the plants often in their daily lives for medicine, cooking and tattooing.

Around 1632, poison ivy seeds were bouncing over the waves toward the British coast. Soon plants were flourishing in some of England's most distinguished gardens.[5, 6] The English were an easy market for this newly discovered "poisoned weed...that can causeth rednesse, itching, and lastly blisters...,"[4] because they have gardening in their blood and cannot help but share a lovely new specimen. I can imagine a garden club member calling to her neighbor, "Beatie, I have a lovely new plant to show you. One slight problem is, you cannot touch it—ever."

Before long, Europe, Africa, Australia, New Zealand and Holland were proud cultivators of plants from the New World—including the one that came with instructions to plant at a distance from garden paths. Holland made use of poison ivy's ability to stabilize soil by planting it along the dikes.

David Douglas was sent to the Northwest around 1830 by Britain's Royal Horticultural Society to see what could be found on the western side of the country. He discovered (and probably experienced) poison oak along the Columbia River between Oregon and Washington. Botany was an exciting occupation in those days. People were literally tripping over plants hitherto unknown in Europe.[5]

By 1850, the delight of poison ivy had long worn off in England and the plant was more or less forgotten—although leftover vines were quietly spreading about old country sheds and such. Around this time, a medical journal published a report that women were developing terrible rashes. Since no cause could be found, it was determined that they were afflicted with hysteria, which resulted in "Hysterical Dermatitis." It seems they were all gardeners—hysterical gardeners.

DANGEROUS OLD-TIME MEDICAL REMEDIES

I suppose I need to include the generic *"Don't do this at home"* statement or some idiot will claim—while being wheeled into the hospital—that he/she saw sulphuric acid or some such remedy recommended in my book.

Various folk remedies for the itch started popping up soon after the colonists hit the coast in the early 1600s. Native Americans used local plants, and herbalists were coming up with suggestions. By the late 1700s not much progress was made by the medical profession—although they were giving it their best shot.

One of the first substances used by physicians as serious medical treatment of poison ivy dermatitis was mercuric chloride (highly poisonous), with the hope that "by its corrosive action on the skin, the poison would be thrown off the affected area." In the 1920s, many of these same chemicals were still being used.[7] My hair is standing on end as I write.

Shortly after exposure, to prevent penetration of the "poison" into the skin, strong solvents were encouraged: ether, chloroform, toluene (severe brain damage from inhaling, death), turpentine (ditto), benzene (ditto) and glacial acetic acid (corrosive).

In 1863, physician Francis Porcher, in all seriousness, wrote that a good accepted remedy was cold applications of acetate of lead. Bloodletting was an option, and opium was mentioned.[8] I can visualize his patients: a group of pale opium addicts dying of lead poisoning wandering the streets at night.

In 1887, James Clark White's suggestions, lacking the "on-the-edge" qualities of Porcher's remedies, were downright dull in comparison. He suggested weak alkaline lotions, carbonate of soda, evaporating lotions of warm or cold water and alcohol, providing the last would "not be too stimulating."[9] Nonetheless, many physicians prescribed the following remedies. Dealing with the rash seemed to be a fight to the death (of the patient).

Old-Time Remedies

Silver nitrate: Toxic and corrosive.

Mercuric chloride: Deadly.

Tincture of iodine: Burns skin.

Lead acetate: Apply as cold as possible. Deadly—sneaks up on you. Called "sugar of lead," it was used as a sweetener. "A bit of sugar of lead in your tea?"

Bromine: Toxic and burns skin.

Sulphuric acid: One of the most corrosive acids.

Arsenic sulphide: Dispensed internally (poison).

Nitric acid: Corrosive, strong acid; explosive with many organic compounds.

Monsel's solution: Comprised of ferrous sulfate, sulfuric acid and nitric acid.

Nitrohydrochloric Acid: Highly corrosive.

Potassium permanganate: Burns skin and stains it dark brown.

Copper sulfate: Corrosive to skin.

Opium, morphine, and cocaine: Develop a rash and your doctor could be your candyman.

Blood root (*Sanguinary canadensis*) destroys skin tissue and produces blisters above inflamed parts.

Formulas

Pulverized borax, carbolic acid, morphine sulphate, powder of acacia.

Morphine sulphate, iodine, carbolic acid.

Lead paint thinned with linseed oil, gunpowder, ammonia, and olive oil.

Ashes of leaves and wood of poison ivy. Dissolve in a milk mixture of sodium chloride, copper sulphate. Leaves of *Datura stramonium* (poisonous).

Make strong lye from wood ashes.

Dissolve a handful of quicklime (caustic) in water. Paint skin. Three or four applications "generally cures."

Sweet spirits of niter: Add one ounce of glycerin and one table spoon carbolic acid to one pint of boiling water.

Dissolve one ounce gum shellac in six ounces of sulphuric ether. Apply to the skin. The ether will evaporate, leaving an elastic, airtight coating of gum. As it peels off, apply more.

Carbolic acid (corrosive to skin), fluidextract of the plant gelsemium (poisonous), glycerin.

Copper sulphate, red mercury, turpentine, lard.

Lead water, opium and mercury.

Benzoic acid and formaldehyde (toxic).

Potassium pernamganate and caustic potash in hot water.

Acacia, morphine sulphate, phenol, borax.

Lead water, opium and mercuric chloride *internally* every three hours.

Lest you suspect that rogue physicians with sadistic tendencies created the foregoing formulas, I offer the following quote from the official organ of the American Dermatological Association in 1918. (Remember, the use of these poisons started back in the late 1700s). "We believe that the purpose of treatment and prophylaxis should be directed only towards the neutralization or destruction of the urushiol... For this purpose, an alkali, nitric acid, and sugar of lead should be applied." [10]

Not all old-time remedies were dangerous and, of course, herbs were used—although a few dangerous ones were popular. Do the words "deadly belladonna" ring a bell? You must admit the above remedies have lots of pizzazz, although the less adventuresome among the public would have been wise to try some of the other recommendations of the time—such as marshmallows and cream, and fresh butter and lemon juice. [7]

HISTORY OF POISON IVY AS A GREAT AMERICAN HEALER

While herbalists were formulating potions to soothe itchy skin, physicians were playing around with the plant to see what in the heck it *cured*. "Poison ivy cures paralysis," according to Frenchman Dr. DuFresnoy in 1788, and in 1793, Englishman Dr. Alderson agreed. Apparently, feeling commences with a sensation of pricking, burning and twitching of the affected parts. This startling news was amended by the late 1800s to mean only the paralysis that follows attacks of rheumatism.[11] But still—is this dramatic or what?

In 1870, John Scudder enthusiastically wrote, "The Rhus is likely to prove one of our most valuable medicines and will be highly prized when its use is learned." Dr. Harvey Felter, also a fan, wrote in 1898, "*Rhus Toxicodendron* (poison ivy) is one of our best medicinal agents. Its range of application, specifically considered, is only excelled by a few drugs."[11] At one point even the U.S. Pharmacopeia considered poison ivy a drug and listed it as *Rhus toxicodendron* in their 1880 and 1890 decennial publications.[12]

Medicinal use of poison ivy was not a flash-in-the-pan fad. In *Materia Medica and Therapeutics* in 1905, Dr. J. Peterson stated, "*Rhus tox* is a valuable remedy when indicated" and was seemingly undaunted by the possible side effects, which included (take a deep breath here) fever, headache, stupefaction, sense of intoxication, burning, nervous twitching, burning in the throat and mouth, thirst, rheumatic pains, cough, nausea, vomiting, chilliness, delirium, drowsiness, stupor, flushed face, dilated pupils, feeble and rapid pulse, hurried respiration, fainting, convulsions, white-coated tongue with small red points on the upper surface of the tip, cough with burning pain in the chest, restlessness, crying out during sleep in children, and—ta-da—itching.[13]

But—hearken to good news. According to the same Dr. J. Peterson, poison ivy (take another deep breath) relieves cerebral engorgement by "increasing the tone of arteries and strengthens the weakened brain." It increases the function of terminal nerve filaments, is an ideal sedative, controls the circulation and is valuable for pneumonia and vomiting. It is used to soothe deep or superficial burning pain and rheumatoid stiffness. The plant also works well for diarrhea and typhoid dysentery, is a "fine remedy" in cholera morbus, and a "valuable agent" in pneumonia, bronchitis, la grippe (flu) and phthisis (tuberculosis). Amazingly, poison ivy is "effective" for sciatica and relieves gastric irritation. It is "of service" in herpes and inflammatory skin afflictions like burning and redness (yep, this was not a typo—it *cures rashes*). And lest we not forget, it also cures rheumatoid paralysis.[11, 14]

It may seem to the skeptical reader that the aforementioned information is a bit over the top—but wait. I have evidence that folks trusted the amazing healing abilities of a plant that should have been called "Super Weed." In 1887, James Clark White wrote, "Great quantities of poison ivy are gathered for medicinal purposes in all parts of the United States. One dealer in North Carolina offers in his stock of native drugs over three hundred pounds of poison ivy leaves."[9]

I must give poison sumac its due. It is not often mentioned because it dwells in standing water, and humans do not saunter around ankle-deep when there is a nice path to walk upon. But it contains the same powerful allergen as poison oak and poison ivy. According to Francis Porcher in 1863, an ointment containing the powerful allergenic resin of this shrubby tree "acts as an astringent when applied to piles."[8] (It shrinks hemorrhoids by gosh.)

The allergenic oils of all three plants are almost identical, so you could make an ointment from any of them. I know the recipe, but I refuse to divulge it because the wildly adventurous out there might actually prepare it and try it out.

SEARCH FOR WHAT CAUSES THE RASH

While herbalists were formulating potions to cure the rash, and physicians were prescribing the herb for every illness under the sun, scientists were playing around with test tubes and poison ivy leaves.

What in blazes does poison ivy contain that is causing the rash?

In America, some botanists and chemists were fascinated by poison ivy. They incorrectly theorized that scentless, colorless and invisible vapors were rising from the plants. Some folks were being affected and others not at all, strangely enough. The vapor theory was not unusual, because it already had been deduced by researchers that all plants give off oxygen in sunlight. One of the researchers, Dr. Ingenbous, had concluded beforehand that all plants emanated poisons in the shade or at night. Therefore, it was not a stretch to conclude that poison ivy produced a virulent poison vapor.

In 1863, botanist Francis Porcher was commissioned to compile information on the plants of the Confederate states. He penned this flamboyant statement on Eastern poison oak:

> "An acrimonious vapor, combined with carbureted hydrogen, exhales from a growing plant of the poison oak during the night. It can be collected in a jar and is capable of inflaming and blistering the skin of persons of excitable constitution, who plunge their arms into it."[8]

In 1858, Joseph Khittel analyzed the resin of poison ivy, at the time called *Rhus toxicodendron*. He concluded that its active principle was an alkaloid. He also believed the oil evaporated from the leaves as they dried, because a dried leaf fallen from the plant contained less of the oil.[15] In fact, during late summer, resin is pulled back into the stems, leaving empty resin canals in the leaves.

In 1865, Professor John M. Maisch conducted a test with litmus paper—simple high school chemistry. The paper turned blue, thus proving the active ingredient was actually an acid. One down, but the scientific community as yet had not deduced that the toxic oil was stable and would not evaporate. Maisch proposed the name *toxicodendric acid* for this "poison." He later stated, "Several persons coming into the room while I was engaged with it were more or less poisoned by the vapors diffused in the room."[9] Oops, he was heading in the wrong direction when talking about "vapors."

In 1887, James White, author of *Dermatitis Venenata*, commented after seeing the above paper: "How far this volatile principle may be carried in the air in a sufficiently concentrated form to produce its peculiar effects upon the skin cannot be exactly stated, but it must vary with the degree of individual susceptibility."[9] He had the last part right, but he was double-oops with the air thing.

These researchers in the late 1800s were baffled because they were thrown off by a bum theory. Slowly, they began to suspect that transference was occurring from one person to another. Some of the folks Dr. Maisch had shaken hands with were developing rashes. "But how shall we explain some of the peculiar phenomena connected with the action of this poison?" the befuddled doctor wrote.[9]

Finally someone started heading in the right direction, but he seemed to be ignored.

Franz Pfaff studied the theories of others, did some experimenting of his own, and in 1897 wrote, "How can the commonly accepted idea be explained that poisoning may occur without actual contact with the poisonous plants when the active principle is a nonvolatile substance?" He proved that oil does not evaporate; therefore, it cannot be floating around to contaminate unsuspecting passersby. He named the oil *toxicodendrol*.[16]

James B. McNair spent many years experimenting with poison oak and studying the earlier experiments of other scientists. He was especially impressed with the work of Franz Pfaff.[16] McNair's book, *Rhus Dermatitis*, published in 1923, is awe-inspiring in what he accomplished, and somewhat of a hoot because of the wild theories people had about this strange rash that sometimes appeared "out of the air."[7]

Does the "poison" evaporate into the air, land on us like a mist, giving us a rash?

McNair used his own experiments and the experiments of others to answer this question once and for all.

EXPERIMENT by McNair.

• Freshly chopped poison oak leaves were distilled by vaporizing liquid and then condensing it back to liquid by cooling the vapor. The resulting fluid failed to cause a rash when applied to a volunteer, proving the oil had not evaporated along with the other moisture. It was not volatile.[7] Apparently ignoring Maisch's "*toxicodendric acid*," and Pfaff's "*toxicodendrol*," McNair renamed the oil "*lobinol*".

EXPERIMENT by von Adelung, 1912 and McNair, 1916.

• Leaves were placed in a combustion tube. Smoke from the burning leaves was blown against a volunteer's skin. Later a rash erupted on the site. When smoke was filtered to block soot, the skin remained unchanged. The conclusion was that the nonvolatile oil was carried in the smoke by soot.[7]

EXPERIMENTS by McNair.

• A small glass with a poison oak leaf taped to the inside was placed on a volunteer's arm. The leaf did not touch the skin, but any vapor would have affected the skin. No rash developed.

• A drop of resin was placed on a volunteer's skin. A small glass was placed over the spot. A rash developed, but only where the sap had touched the skin.

• Poison oak resin was placed on a volunteer's skin. After a rash developed, a piece of skin in that area was removed and viewed under a microscope. The oil had not penetrated as quickly as it would have if the oil were volatile. (Volatile poisons like petroleum and benzyl rapidly penetrate into the tissues and diffuse there.)[7]

By this time, at least two researchers had proven the "poisonous" oil was stable and not volatile.

Poisoning seems to occur without touching the plant, but how?

When James McNair finished the above research, he worked on this next perplexing mystery. A few researchers had already tackled the problem:

In 1882, Burrill speculated that bacteria caused the poison ivy rash. His reasoning:

1. Only *some* people catch it.
2. The rash takes hours or days to occur, suggesting incubation.
3. Germicidal agents, specifically carbolic acid, seemed to help cure the rash.

Under the microscope Burrill observed what he described as "minute spherical bodies" that he incorrectly identified as microorganisms. He believed they were inside the stems and on the surface of the leaves. Oddly, he made no attempt to culture the bodies to see if they multiplied. It's simple—take a petri dish, add a mixture that resembles bland Jell-O, wait awhile and the proof is in the pudding, so to speak. Live microorganisms would multiply, and the result? Definitely not dessert.

In 1895 the doctor humbly admitted he might have been wrong. He seems to have aborted his experiments rather suddenly. His own arms were test models and he had experienced, as he called it, "very serious results."[7]

A few years after Burrill's report, the "spherical bodies" were determined to be part of the plant structure.

1902: K. Schwalbe theorized that tiny hairs on the leaves, called trichomes (barely seen by eye), were carrying the toxic substance and then broke off to be carried by the wind to unsuspecting people. Aided by work done by Rost and Gilg in 1912, McNair destroyed that theory with yet more innovative experiments.[7]

1904: S. Hubbord—and in 1906, A. Hadden—speculated that insects trotted around on the leaves, picked up the "poison" on their wee feet and then took an afternoon stroll on a nearby arm, thereby transferring the toxic stuff to the victim. Whaddaya think, credible? [7]

1912: Von Adelung thought the answer was toxic pollen being blown about by the wind. There's a flaw to this theory. Not sporting the little wings that assist other pollens to become airborne, poison oak and poison ivy pollens are very sticky and remain in the flower, awaiting insects.[7]

1916: C. Frost considered "Rhus dermatitis" a "systemic infectious disease" because of organisms he found on samples of leaves. Introduction of his cultured bacteria to a test person produced no rash, which he handily explained by theorizing that the culturing mechanism weakened the bacteria. His arguments:

1. There was an incubation period. (This is a *delayed* type of allergy.)[7]

2. Some people were "immune." (Persons without an allergy will not react.)

3. Rashes were often in areas untouched by the plant. (The oil is accidentally smeared around.)[7]

McNair charged into the battle in 1923 in his book *Rhus Dermatitis*. ***It's a chemical reaction from touching the oil, not those harebrained theories, you idiots.*** Just kidding, but we know he was *thinking* that.[7]

Even with all his research, McNair did not connect what he was researching with a new theory that had been developed in 1906 by Viennese pediatrician, Baron Clemens von Pirquet. The clever physician came up with the concept that a response to outside substances such as dust, pollen and so forth, might be causing some puzzling symptoms. He named the response "allergy."[17]

One big reason all those scientists were bamboozled was because they had no concept of "delayed contact hypersensitivity," a type of allergic reaction caused by oil in the resin of poison oak, poison ivy and their kin. The key words here are, *the rash is delayed*—for hours or days.

McNair's book *Rhus Dermatitis* was written in 1923, but he was not going in the allergy direction. He was thinking that to gain tolerance you needed to become immune—as against chicken pox, for example. He wrote, "Judging by the evidence at present, there seem to be two forms of immunity, natural and acquired...Persons are frequently found who are immune to lobinol (his name for the allergenic oil) when it is applied in the same concentration and condition as it exists in the sap of the plant, but when applied in a more concentrated form these persons are affected by it."[7]

Does the fluid in the blisters contain the "toxic" ingredient?

James White, committed researcher that he was, gave himself a case of poison ivy and experimented with the blisters on his arm by applying the clear fluid from them to the arm of another gentleman, who was greatly relieved when nothing happened.[9]

Strangely, this last information failed to spread like wildfire, or even a slow burn. To this day a good number of the population believes that their blisters contain the "poison oil" and that they are a ticking time bomb for anyone else who touches the blister fluid. Yuck.

References

1. Nie, Ze-Long, et al. 2009. "Phylogenetic Analysis of Toxicodendron: Anacardiaceas and Its Biogeographic Implications on the Evolution of North Temperate and Tropical Intercontinental Disjunctions." *Journal of Systematics and Evolution* 47(5):416-430.

2. Pell, Susan. 2011. Plant Molecular Systematist. E-mail correspondence.

3. Wen, Jun. 2011? Research Botanist. E-mail correspondence.

4. Smith, John. 1624. *General Historie of Virginia, New England, and the Sumer Isles.* Fifth Book.

5. Anderson, Thomas E. 1995. *The Poison Ivy, Oak and Sumac Book.* Action Circle, CA.

6. Gillis, William T. 1971. "The Systematics and Ecology of Poison Ivy and the Poison Oaks (Toxicodendron, *Anacardiaceae*)." *Rhodora*, vol. 73.

7. McNair, James B. 1923. *Rhus Dermatitis*. The University of Chicago Press.

8. Porcher, Francis P. 1863. *Resources of the Southern Fields and Forests, Medical, Economical and Agricultural*. Steam Power Press, VA.

9. White, James Clark. 1887. *Dermatitis Venenata*.

10. MacKee, George M., ed. 1918. *Journal of Cutaneous Diseases Including Syphilis*, vol. 36.

11. Felter, Harvey Wickes, and John Uri LLoyd. 1898. *King's American Dispensatory*.

12. US Pharmacopedia. 2010. Staff phone interview and e-mail.

13. Peterson, Fred J. 1905. *The Materica Medica and Clinical Therapeutics*. Self-published, CA.

14. Scudder, John M. 1870. *Specific Medication and Specific Medicines*. Wilstach, Baldwin & Co. Printers.

15. Khittel, Joseph. 1858. *American Journal of Pharmacy*.

16. Pfaff, Franz. 1897. "On the Active Principle of Rhus Toxicodendron and Rhus Venenata." *Journal of Experimental Medicine* 2(2):181-195.

17. Mitchell, John, and Arthur Rock. 1979. *Botanical Dermatology: Plants Injurious to the Skin*. Greenslash Ltd., Canada.

Burt's childhood ballet lessons
finally pay off!

Chapter 6

THE ALLERGENIC OIL ISOLATED

CHEMISTRY OF THE ALLERGENIC OIL—URUSHIOL

The big whoop-de-do is all about urushiol. It's one of the most powerful allergens known. A tiny amount—as low as 50 micrograms of purified urushiol—on the skin will produce an allergic response within the immune system in 80 percent of people who have never been exposed.[1] Later, the amount of oil exposure to create a rash will be dependent upon whether a person developed a low or high sensitivity to the oil, the quantity of oil that penetrated the skin, and the type of skin exposed. The palm of the hand is thick and tough, whereas the skin on the inside of the wrist is delicate.

While Americans curse poison oak and poison ivy, the Japanese carefully tend a tree with almost the same allergenic oil. Forests of the Japanese lacquer tree they call "kiurushi" (or urushi ki) are tapped for the resin, called "urushi." This resin is processed to produce the lacquer used to create the beautiful lacquerware of which they are so proud. Urushi contains a whopping 60 to 75 percent urushiol, 5 percent carbohydrate, 1 percent soluble protein and 1 percent enzymes. The rest is water.

Around 1915, Japanese researchers identified the compound in the resin urushi that causes the allergic reaction and named it "urushiol." It is now agreed that the word urushiol refers not only to the kiurushi tree (*Toxicodendron verniciluum*), but also to the allergenic oil in the resin of the rest of the members of the genus, because the oils of all these plants are closely related.[2]

There are three physical qualities of urushiol that are important.

1. Volatility (rate of evaporation at normal temperatures): Although early studies in the 1800s on urushiol were bogged down by an assumption that it was extremely volatile; it is one of the heaviest, least volatile oils in the plant kingdom. When poison oak or poison ivy plants are burned, instead of evaporating, tiny droplets of urushiol rise on soot into the air—a danger to anyone downwind.

2. Solubility in water: Urushiol is an oil—a mixture of closely related phenolic lipids (a kind of fat) that is one of the least water soluble of dermatitis-causing plant products. It can have a strong taste and smell.[3]

3. Solubility in fat: Urushiol is extremely soluble in solvents and fats, which gives it the ability to be absorbed quickly by skin, thereby activating the immune system.

4. The boiling point of urushiol is 200° to 210°F, not that any of you would have occasion to boil up a cup.

The opaque or clear resin (opacity depends upon the amount of sap released with the resin) that contains urushiol, seeps from wounds in the plant tissues, and on exposure to oxygen slowly oxidizes with the assistance of the enzyme laccase (not to be confused with lactase). The color soon turns tan, then brown, and within a few hours to twelve hours or so, depending on air temperature and humidity, a hard black membrane is formed. This process is called polymerization. The hard membrane is still allergenic at this stage, and could be so for a good long while, especially if the atmosphere is dry. Oxidation is of great importance. When complete, it almost eliminates the allergenic capability of the urushiol.[4] The key word is "almost"—a lacquer bowl, buried for two hundred years, gave a rash to an archaeologist who handled it. In a warm, moist environment, oxidation speeds up, but in a protected, dry spot, oxidation is sloooow.

Urushiol separated from the resin has a thick, sticky consistency. This is another reason it can be difficult to remove from skin.[5]

In the language of chemistry according to *Webster's Collegiate Dictionary*, urushiol is "a mixture of catechol derivatives with saturated or unsaturated side chains of 15 or 17 carbon atoms." Each species of *Toxicodendron* has a different mixture of saturated and unsaturated molecules. Catechols are what stimulate the allergic reaction. For example, poison ivy mostly contains a mixture of pentadecylcatechols (with 15 carbon side chains), while poison oak contains a mixture of heptadecylcatechols (with 17 carbon side chains).[6] That's okay, I don't understand it either.

Many substances with the potential to be an allergen in humans also are irritating to the skin. It is believed that urushiol is an irritant. Two medical dictionaries I consulted described urushiol as such, but poison ivy researcher Albert Kligman disagreed, based on having applied root, stem, and leaf sap to nonsensitive persons without noticing any irritation before the rash appeared."[7] I timidly disagree with the good doctor, based only on my own arms. When applying poison oak resin drops from a cut stem to my inner arms while testing remedies, each drop immediately caused a tiny raised bump that felt slightly irritated for about twenty minutes. The small allergic reaction did not appear for about sixteen hours. Obviously I am no longer very sensitive to poison oak, but I paid my dues during my younger years. And how.

A difference between the chemistry of the urushiols of the Japanese lacquer tree and those of the American Toxicodendrons is that *our* urushiols do not have the hardening properties for high-quality lacquerware. In a couple of months, a nice shiny black coat of poison oak oil would develop a powdery, rough, gray surface outside, but kept inside from the sun it will stay shiny, if not oriental-lacquer quality.

Rats, there goes the possibility for an American manufacturing business—just because our poison oak and poison ivy plants are not up to snuff. If only they were commercially viable and harvested beyond their sustainability—they would become an endangered species in no time. Then you could saunter around the countryside completely safe, although here and there one would notice little fenced patches planted in a feeble attempt to reintroduce these true natives to the landscape.

To sum it up, "urushiol" is a general term for a group of related compounds in the genus *Toxicodendron* that cause the allergic rash. The molecular structures vary a little bit, but a person allergic to one will be allergic to the others.

NOTE: I use the term "resin," whereas some writers use "sap," or "latex." Jean Langenheim, author of *Plant Resins*, says urushiol is a phenolic resin.[8]

References

1. Epstein, William L. "Occupational Poison Ivy and Oak Dermatitis." *Dermatologic Clinics* 12(3):511-516.

2. Baer, Harold. 1986. "Chemistry and Immunochemistry of Poisonous *Anacardiaceae*." *Clinics in Dermatology* 4(2):152-159.

3. Crosby, Donald G. 2004. *The Poisoned Weed*. Oxford University Press, NY.

4. Keeler, Richard, and Anthony T. Tu. 1983. *Plant and Fungal Toxins*. Marcel Inc., Dekker, NY.

5. Choi, Ju-Youn, Chang-Soo Park, Jongoh Choi, Hyangshuk Rhim, and Jae Chun Heung. 2001. "Cytotoxic Effects of Urushiol on Human Ovarian Cancer Cells." *Journal of Microbiology and Biotechnology* 11:399-405.

6. Armstrong, W.P., and W.L. Epstein. 1995. "Poison Oak: More than Just Scratching the Surface." *HerbalGram* (American Botanical Council).

7. Kligman, Albert M. 1957. "Poison Ivy (Rhus) Dermatitis: An Experimental Study." Archives of Dermatology 77(2):149-180.

8. Langenheim, Jean H. 2003. *Plant Resins: Chemistry, Evolution, Ecology, and Ethnobotany*. Timber Press, Portland, OR.

Chapter 7

HOW
ALLERGIES
WORK

WHAT IS AN ALLERGY?

Our immune system is our protector, our warrior heading out to do battle with those pesky viruses and bacteria that are shot out of some guy's mouth just as you happen to turn your head his way. "Achoo," he goes, as your hair is blown back. "Not to worry," says your immune system, and the next day finds you hale and hearty— or not.

An allergy, on the other hand, is the immune system trying hard to keep you upright and perky, but it's heading down the wrong path with a vengeance, sending out the big guns against innocent bystanders. The symptoms you have to put up with are the aftermath of the carnage. *"A poison oak and ivy rash is an allergic reaction (sensitization) and susceptibility is genetically controlled."*[1]

Among a long list, here are some of the harmless things your immune system might consider to be an enemy (allergen).

Plant resins: Many of the family *Anacardiaceae*, especially the genus *Toxicodendron*, including the *species* poison oak, poison ivy and poison sumac.

Animal products: Dog dander (dandruff) and dog saliva.

Insect products: Dust mite excrement (yes, mite doo doo in your rug).

Prescription drugs: Penicillin.

Foods: Strawberries, peanuts, shrimp, and many other foods.

Insect sting: Bees, wasps, hornets.

Mold spores: A leak under the sink.

Plant pollen: Ragweed, birch, juniper, grasses.

Plant products: Skin cream.

Occupational dust and chemicals: Hair-perming solutions, for example.

Latex: Latex gloves.

Metal: Nickel jewelry.

Chemicals: In fabrics, skin-care products, medicines.

Your body: Rheumatoid arthritis, Crohn's disease, multiple sclerosis.

Ways to contact an allergen

Eating or drinking.

Breathing into lungs.

Injection by a syringe or insect.

Contact with skin.

Saddest of all, something you are always in contact with—your own body. You cannot run away from it, throw it out, sweep it up or take it off.

Symptoms

Various types of skin rash (dermatitis).

Trouble breathing (anaphylaxis, could be deadly).

Runny nose.

Digestive problems.

Joint pain.

Ear infections.

Spacey feeling.

Flu symptoms.

Lung problems.

TYPES OF ALLERGIES
Hypersensitivities

An allergic reaction might be a small red spot on your forearm or a tremendously strong response toward a little bit of nothing much. Kind of like Russian roulette—Click or **Bang!**

Allergies range from having to blow your nose right after you pass a truck hauling alfalfa bales, to being allergic to almost everything you come across in your daily life—like my stepmother who could eat only some nuts, seeds and a few fruits and vegetables. She wore a facemask when leaving home. My father was the dinner chef, and the fact that she was forty years his junior seemed to make up for his lack of culinary options. She could drink wine, which certainly helped flesh out the menu and kept them in good spirits.

THE FOUR TYPES OF ALLERGIC REACTIONS
Whether a reaction is immediate or delayed can aid in determining the type of allergy it is.

1. TYPE I HYPERSENSITIVITY
Immediate type: No more than thirty minutes for a reaction.

Examples: Allergic contact Eczema—skin inflammation, but not the same immune chemistry as poison oak or ivy dermatitis. Hay fever—nose and sinus. Hives—raised red and itching patches. Anaphylactic shock—airway closes off. Can cause death within minutes.[2, 3]

2. TYPE II HYPERSENSITIVITY
Delayed type: Hours to a day for a reaction.

Antigens are the patient's own cell surfaces, or foreign antigens absorbed into the patient's cells.

Examples: Blood transfusion reaction, organ transplants, some drugs.[2, 3]

3. TYPE III HYPERSENSITIVITY

Delayed type: Hours to a day for a reaction.

Examples: Rheumatoid arthritis, Crohn's disease, some food allergies.[2, 3]

This next immune response is the type caused by poison oak, poison ivy, poison sumac and their relatives

4. TYPE IV HYPERSENSITIVITY. Also called allergic contact dermatitis, delayed type hypersensitivity, cell mediated hypersensitivity and cell mediated immune response.

Delayed type: Typically one to three days for a reaction.

This reaction does not involve antibodies. Instead, various types of white blood cells are activated (T cells, eosinophils, macrophages, neutrophils and others). Enzymes and chemicals are released, causing tissue damage.

Examples: The oil in the resin of poison oak, poison ivy and their relatives, and many other plants (plants may be in products such as skin cream, latex gloves), dyes, plastic, rubber, insecticide, fungi, chemicals, metal jewelry.

Only certain people will develop Type IV allergic contact dermatitis; others will be unaffected. Susceptibility is genetically controlled.

Symptoms: Skin inflammation, blisters, intense itching, burning. In the case of poison oak and poison ivy rash, liver, kidney, respiratory and digestive system injury can occur, and very seldom—death.

The following have a similar immune chemistry: Transplant rejection, diabetes mellitus, insulin dependent (type 1), symptoms of leprosy, the test for tuberculosis, the rash of some viruses. Herpes, measles and smallpox are examples.[2, 3, 4]

TYPES OF RASH (DERMATITIS) FROM PLANTS
Allergic and Nonallergic

You are sauntering along a path in the country. Suddenly your arm is wildly itching and stinging—yeow! "Must be poison oak. I spied some awhile back," your friend offers. Nope. A poison oak rash is a contact type of dermatitis, but it is a *delayed* type.

Contact dermatitis can be an allergic or nonallergic reaction. It's an inflammation of skin.

There are four types of reactions that can occur as a result of exposure to plants or plant-derived products (certain skin creams, for example). Your immune system may be trying to start a war (an allergic reaction), or there might be something in the plant that damages the skin without the immune system becoming involved.

1. ALLERGIC CONTACT DERMATITIS
Allergic type of reaction—delayed.

This is a Type IV hypersensitivity already discussed under the heading "Types of allergies." Poison oak, poison ivy and poison sumac rashes are in this category and are the prime offenders in the United States.

The reaction is delayed after contact. Usually at least four hours goes by before symptoms occur. It often takes up to twelve hours and occasionally a few days. The rash will last two or three weeks, but the skin usually heals well. Expect mild to horrible skin inflammation. Weeping blisters and continuous itching is not unusual.[5]

2. IMMEDIATE CONTACT DERMATITIS (*contact urticaria*).

Nonallergic type of reaction—immediate (reaction is less than thirty minutes from exposure).

Nettles: Touch the plant—immediate stinging fireworks on your skin.

Hives: You can feel them rising up. Eating certain foods like strawberries, peanuts and also many nonbotanicals, like drugs, can cause hives.[5]

3. PHYTOPHOTODERMATITIS
Nonallergenic type of reaction—delayed.

Touch a particular plant and then go into the sun. Chemicals cause skin to redden and swell in one or two days and burn like the dickens. Huge blisters may appear, but it doesn't itch.[5]

4. IRRITANT CONTACT DERMATITIS
Nonallergenic type of reaction—immediate.

The skin is affected mechanically or chemically. It becomes inflamed.

Mechanical: Rose thorns, spines on cacti, leaf hairs of comfrey, and more.

Chemical: Contains irritant substances—hot peppers and poinsettia, for example.

Summing up, there are a number of ways plants or plant-containing products can affect your skin:

Delayed allergic reaction that takes days to show up. (Poison oak or poison ivy).

Immediate nonallergic reaction.

Delayed nonallergic reaction that needs both a plant chemical and sunlight.

Skin puncture or a chemical irritant. Those darned rose bushes get me every time.[5]

References

1. Rietschel, Robert L. 2008. *Fisher's Contact Dermatitis*. BC Decker, Inc.

2. Sompayrac, Lauren. 2008. *How The Immune System Works*. Blackwell Pub., MA.

3. Joneja, Janice Vickerstaff. 1990. *Understanding Allergy Sensitivity and Immunity: A Comprehensive Guide*. Rutgers University Press.

4. Kerwin, Edward M., MD. Allergist. 2010. Interview. Oregon.

5. Avalos, Javier, and Howard I. Maibach, eds. 2000. *Dermatologic Botany*. CRC Press, NY.

Mrs. Peabody's lovely fall bouquet was *NOT* a big hit at the garden club luncheon.

Chapter 8

EXPLAINING THE RASH

STRUCTURE OF THE SKIN

Skin is the stretchy bag around bones, muscles, organs and nerves. It is the first line of defense.

Our skin is actually an organ, like the spleen or heart. In fact, it is the largest organ—up to 10 percent of our body weight—and is the only organ you can inspect easily as compared to, for example, trying to check your liver for bruises after a nasty fall.

Skin is composed of three layers

1. EPIDERMIS: The epidermis is what we see—smooth baby bottoms and wrinkled eighty-year-old grandfathers. It meets the environment head on, gets beat up, and is constantly being replaced.

The protective barrier, which is mainly on the surface—is made up of lipids, water, sebum (triglycerides and cholesterol) and sweat. The allergenic oil urushiol can easily penetrate this barrier and move between the cells through the lipid and water mixture (intercellular matrix) to the lower layers of the epidermis.

What we normally call *pores* are actually *follicles*. Pores produce sweat. You can't see them, and they don't open or close. Follicles have sebaceous glands attached to them. Some have hair and some don't. They expand and contract a bit. Urushiol can make its way down the follicle, through the sebaceous gland and into the lower skin areas, and its journey possibly could be aided by heat, which causes the follicles to expand and oil to flow easier.

The epidermis has four layers

(1). Stratum corneum: The thick layer that's out there for the public to see. Commonly called the "horny layer," these overlapping dead cells are related to horn, hair and bird feathers. Give us a few million years of evolution and we might be flying to work.

(2). Stratum lucidum: Sometimes called the "transparent layer," these cells are designed to reduce friction and shear forces between the corneum and granulosum cell layers on palms of hands and soles of feet. Normally they are seen in thick epidermis, especially the hands and feet.

(3). Stratum granulosum (granular cell layer): Replaces cells as the top layer wears away.

(4). Stratum spinosum: Keratin is produced here—a fibrous protein that is pushed up to the surface to toughen the skin.

Important to the allergic response, and in this layer, are Langerhans cells. They wander around and, after being alerted by other cells on guard, initiate the beginning of the immune system's response to antigens (poison oak oil, for example) that are passing through the skin. Water may not get through, but oil does—like a ghost through a wall.

(5). Stratum basale (basal layer): This deepest layer of the epidermis sits on the dermis and is the source of replacement cells that slowly migrate to the top of the pile to face the environment. "Come on world, give it your best shot." Having been supplied with blood from the dermis below, they slowly die as they migrate farther from the blood supply.

2. DERMIS: The dermis is the middle part of the skin and contains collagen and elastin fibers for skin elasticity. The dermis can be very thin on eyelids, and very thick on soles of feet. This area of the skin is important in the allergic response. Mast cells hang out close to the blood vessels of the dermis. They contain histamine, heparin, and other chemicals that are inflammatory, and also act on blood vessels. Sebaceous glands and follicles are based in this

area. The dermis is the first layer to deliver nourishing blood and lymph, and the first layer with nerves to transmit heat, cold, pain, pressure and touch. Unfortunately, nerves also convey the sensation of itching—which they do quite well.

3. HYPODERMIS: Good ole fat and loose connective tissue. This layer contains the major blood vessels of the skin and provides shock absorption and insulation.[1, 2, 3. Covers whole subchapter.]

PROGRESSION OF THE RASH
How bad can it get, and how long will it last?

OIL ON YOUR SKIN
The picnic in the woods was heavenly. Unfortunately, your immune system is in an uproar because of a lovely plant you brushed against, picked for a fall bouquet or used for toilet paper in an "oops, I gotta go—now" scenario.

Urushiol, the allergenic oil, has been on your skin for over ten minutes and has penetrated the epidermis (outer layer of skin). Your immune system blared out a warning and the troops are busy mobilizing. They believe they are galloping to your rescue. Talk about mistakes.

CONTAMINATION
How bad will the rash be? It depends.
The allergenic oil absorbs into skin quite readily through the lipid area between cells. Thick skin on palms of hands or soles of feet slows or stops penetration of the allergenic oil. That's why you will often get a rash between your fingers, but not on your palms.

• A *large* amount of the oil will stimulate the immune system to ramp up and create symptoms sooner than if exposure was minimal.

- How allergic are you? The highly allergic can expect a reaction in less time than the mildly allergic.

- Was a barrier product applied beforehand? Studies show these can be very helpful in reducing oil/skin contact.

- You have up to ten minutes to remove the allergenic oil before it starts to tickle the immune system—unless you are extremely sensitive. In that case, you've got three minutes tops. The longer you wait, the more oil will be absorbed and the worse the rash.

- The immune system will speed up its reaction time if you are re-exposed to the allergen before the current rash heals.

Onset of rash: Six to twenty-four hours is normal, because it takes awhile for the immune system to unlock the war chest, but it might take four to six days. Having just written what is generally accepted as *normal*, there is always an example of an outlaw allergy breaking all the rules. A researcher applied five dabs of plant resin on his forearm. Three areas started itching on day four, one on day six, and the last rash held off for a full fifteen days.[4] During the time I was extremely sensitive, my rash would begin to erupt the day after contamination.

Worsening: Seven to ten days is normal. Sometimes longer.

Recovering: Seven to ten days is normal. Sometimes longer.

Average time from beginning to end: Two to three weeks, often longer—especially for the extremely allergic person. It can seem forever, but don't rule out the chance you could have recontaminated yourself from tools, clothes, etc. Did you hug your dog?[5]

A minor rash

A minor rash will appear later and heal sooner than a serious rash. The area will begin to itch as the skin reddens and swells. Tiny bumps are common and will release small amounts of clear plasma. The skin often has a rough, abraded look.

A serious rash

Assuming you got a good dollop of the allergenic oil or are extremely sensitive, you will get what science calls an "erythematous papulovesicular" rash that is intensely pruritic. Lesions form, and later bullae, that quickly erupt, releasing plasma. Translation: The skin begins to redden, small raised blisters form, and it all itches to beat the band. Skin tissue has been damaged, and clear plasma seeps from blood vessels, forming large blisters (that do not contain the allergenic oil). The blisters soon burst, and fluid flowing over the skin forms a crust that continues to grow, like cooling lava from a half-hearted volcano.

A very serious rash

Some sufferers end up in the hospital when symptoms become overwhelming. Before cortisone was marketed, little could be done to stop the process and the highly allergic rode it out. Besides a horrendous rash, other symptoms might include fever, chills, headache, drowsiness, nausea, vomiting and toxic effects on liver and kidneys.[6] Researcher Albert Kligman felt that the onset of gastrointestinal reactions was "against an allergic origin," and thought maybe other exudations of the plants contain additional substances that would cause the symptoms. Some other phenolic resins that are used medicinally do cause undesirable stomach symptoms and are diluted before administering.[7]

In 1887, James Clark White dramatically summed up the whole experience. "The effect produced by these various agents is to excite an inflammatory process in the cutaneous tissues of all possible degrees of intensity"[8]

STRANGE HAPPENINGS MIGHT OCCUR

1. During a serious outbreak, the immune system seems to become overstimulated—"Yeehaw!" Besides the basic rash, small itchy inflammations sometimes pop up in areas of sensitive skin that the plant oil never touched—like armpits, inside the forearms or behind the knees. The self-satisfied message to you from your im-

mune system is something like "Fear not, I will protect your arm-pits, forearms, and knees—*from nothing*."

2. A newly healed rash might experience a flare-up weeks later in response to a new rash at another site or from a patch test. There seems to be a chemical memory. It is suspected that T cells hanging around the old site are jarred into action from sensing the new outbreak.[9]

3. When a serious rash has healed, there is often a period of a few months with no reaction from exposure to the plant resin. One theory is that the regulatory T cells in the skin that were mobilized to tone down the allergic reaction are still collected at the sites and will respond easily to any whiff of the allergen in the system. Another theory is that the *chemicals* from the immune system's regulatory (suppressor) reaction are still in the system and have enough potency to continue suppressing.[10, 11]

4. A few people have mentioned to me that after a horrendous childhood rash, they never had another response from exposure to poison oak or poison ivy or, if so, the rash was minor.

DOES SCRATCHING MAKE THE RASH WORSE?

It seems to many of us that when we scratch, the rash spreads.

1. Spreading the blister fluid by scratching is messy—ugh! But the fluid only contains clear plasma from the blood.

2. Some folks are certain that scratching increases the production of histamine and other itch-producing chemicals. Not from what I have read by researchers.

3. Scratching will increase the likelihood of infection.

4. If even a tiny amount of the allergenic oil remains on the surface of your skin, scratching will spread the oil, which will cause the rash to spread.

5. Studies on itch have shown that scratching can sometimes reduce the itching for awhile, but not for long.[12]

Some of you stoically refrain from scratching horrible rashes. Others, like me, last about ten minutes—even with puny rashes. From my experience, it seems that scratching possibly will give you more agony in the long run by adding to the inflammation, but how can a weakling such as I calmly advise you to twiddle your thumbs when your whole nerve network is dancing the fandango on your skin?

DOES AGE MATTER?

The highest degree of sensitization usually occurs in childhood after infancy and then becomes less intense with aging, regardless of continued exposure. There are always exceptions, and many seniors suffer from their allergies. Some folks have become extremely wary throughout the years, evading the plants with a well-tuned poison oak or poison ivy sensor system. And of course, many seniors don't get out like they used to.[7, 13]

DO ALL RACES HAVE THE SAME CAPABILITY TO DEVELOP AN ALLERGY?

This is a bit tricky. For instance, the Chinese, Japanese and Koreans use lacquer-painted products in many aspects of their life and, because the lacquer is from the Japanese lacquer tree, a close relative to poison oak and poison ivy, they will test very low for sensitivity to poison oak and poison ivy on patch tests. If their children are American born, they will test normal for Americans. Dark-skinned people are less apt to be sensitive to poison oak and poison ivy than Caucasians.[7]

COMPLICATIONS

1. Scratching causes mechanical disruption of the skin, increasing water loss and exposing skin nerve endings to dryness, which causes nerve endings to itch like a bad sunburn on top of the histamine-caused itch. Constant scratching also can put the skin at risk for impetigo, a bacterial infection.[14]

2. There is a condition called "immune complex disease" that may occur during an extreme case of poison oak or poison ivy der-

matitis. This can cause a life-threatening kidney disease if medical attention is not sought.[9]

3. Darkening of skin pigmentation after healing is sometimes seen on dark-skinned individuals. This is not a permanent condition.

4. The infamous "black spot" is a black tattoo-like spot wherein a glob of urushiol (the allergenic oil) oxidizes, turning the skin black. Although it sounds ominous (tattooed for life?), a Japanese lacquer painter told me she removes the black spots with a pumice stone.

5. After the first eruption, the circumference often expands or new rashes develop. Folks often fear the mess will never heal, as they unknowingly recontaminate themselves.

OTHER SOURCES OF CONTACT

Wildfire smoke

Wildfire fighters and gardeners burning the plants are in danger of inhaling small droplets of the oil sailing along on soot. The immune reaction could cause inflammation in the throat and lungs, leading to a life-threatening situation.

Eating a leaf

Not a good idea. Apparently Native Americans chewed poison oak or poison ivy leaves to decrease sensitivity. Exceed the tolerance of your immune system and not only is it probable you will break out here and there, but the oil also will travel through your digestive system mostly intact and create a rash as it passes through the exit door. "Good-bye and good luck."

One spring, a good friend of mine chewed up a small leaflet every day for a week, hoping to develop a tolerance. Blisters formed on her gums. She saw no connection with her new "diet" and visited her dentist thinking she had a gum infection. He commented that if he didn't know better, he would think she had a poison oak reaction in her mouth. Uh, yup.

WHAT IS THE WORST SCENARIO?

The worst scenario is immune complex disease ending in death. I found a medical study from 1948 discussing two *possible* deaths from serious cases of poison ivy that damaged the kidneys. The physicians did not have enough data to make definite conclusions.[15]

I also have an interesting paper written in 1951 wherein the authors described recently witnessing a fatal reaction and a near-fatal reaction caused by physicians administering an extract of poison ivy (unrelated to the highly diluted homeopathic formulas) as they attempted to cure the *existing* poison ivy rashes of their patients. Yikes! The dermatitis expanded to become extremely serious and kidney inflammation followed.[16]

In 1945 the Council on Pharmacy and Chemistry of the American Medical Association denounced the use of the allergen (poison ivy oil) to cure an existing rash *caused* by poison ivy.[16] This can send the immune system into overdrive. If you have an existing poison oak or poison ivy rash, do your best to prevent recontamination.

Inhaling the allergenic oil on soot from a fire is considered possibly highly dangerous, but I never found a discussion or confirmation of a death from throat or lung involvement.

For dangerous cases of poison oak or poison ivy, intravenous prednisone is administered in the hospital. This corticosteroid will put a halt to the immune reaction by shutting it down; the side effect being that the individual is then susceptible to infection.

COULD SOMETHING ELSE CAUSE THE RASH?

The word "rash" is a general term that describes any visible skin outbreak, from tiny mottled patches hardly noticeable to festering blisters covering broad areas of the body, seeming to move like the blob—changing perfectly nice facial features into Quasimodo-like disfigurations.

There are many possible causes for a rash. Is it really from poison oak or poison ivy?

Other plants that cross-react: Besides other members of the genus *Toxicodendron*, all of which contain the allergen urushiol, there are three other botanicals with allergenic chemicals that are *not* related, but that cross-react with urushiol. Strangely enough, if you are allergic to poison oak or poison ivy, you are probably allergic to all of the other three. Mango rash usually manifests in a rash around the mouth from eating unpeeled mangos. Chances are you will never be exposed to the oil between the two layers of a cashew nut but if you are, don't touch it. The fruit of the female ginkgo tree is another cross-reactor, but most ginkgo trees sold are male, which do not produce fruit, and the leaves don't seem to be much of a threat, if at all.

Anything different lately? A recent hike in the country perhaps? Previous skin disorders, food or drug allergies, other friends or family with a similar condition, recent travels, illnesses, exposure to new cleaning products or other chemicals? Have you tried a new skin-care product lately?

Changes in the rash: Did the rash develop quickly, or progress slowly? Remember, a poison oak or poison ivy rash is a "delayed" allergic reaction. This means it will take over six hours or days to appear.

Symptoms: Does your rash hurt, burn, sting, throb? Pain takes a back seat to unbelievable itching with a serious poison oak and poison ivy rash. Fever, gastric disturbances and general malaise are possible, but uncommon with these rashes.

Location of the rash: Is the breakout in one spot, here-and-there, or covering the whole body? A poison oak or poison ivy rash usually seems to be moving—expanding or even jumping around.

Rash medication: Medication may be causing an allergic reaction, especially if the rash has not begun to fade after two weeks. For example, a patient self-medicated with neomycin when it seemed his rash became infected. A huge rash appeared over the poison oak rash—an allergic reaction to the cream.[17]

Even ingredients in products designed to stop the itch can cause a rash. Antihistamine in a cream or even calamine lotion are examples.

WHAT A POISON OAK AND POISON IVY RASH WILL *NOT* DO

The rash will never cover the entire surface of the body.

The rash will seldom arise on palms or soles of feet.

The rash will never affect your nervous system like shingles.

The rash will not have a distinct unchanging shape.

The rash will not suddenly appear within a few minutes of contact with the plants.

Would it make sense for an allergist to do a patch test?

In 1795 a Dr. Fontana was possibly the first researcher to conduct a patch test. He applied a cut leaf of poison ivy to his own skin.

Around 1920, patch testing was beginning to be used in the U.S. When I was tested, my allergist placed dabs of various allergens on my back. Mold created a reaction on my skin, showing I was allergic. I now receive injections of mold each month.

Researcher Albert Kligman wrote, "Patch tests may be quite misleading...when the test concentration greatly exceeds that of natural circumstance.[11]

Indiscriminately patching a patient with poison oak or poison ivy oil is not a good idea. Eighty percent of the population will test positive to these plants. Testing a nonsensitive patient with the active ingredient in poison oak or poison ivy might exceed their tolerance level and then *create* an allergy. A family physician can usually recognize the "signature" of a poison oak or poison ivy rash anyway.

Now that you have assessed all aspects of the rash, let's assume you believe it is from poison oak or poison ivy.

The following might be mistaken for poison oak or poison ivy because these rashes also leave you scratching (in order of most likely to least likely to be mistaken).

Scorpion weed: Genus Phacelia. There are around two hundred species of these plants native to North America. Many have tiny hairs that irritate the skin, but there are at least twelve species that have been shown to contain an allergen that produces a rash that is hard to distinguish from a poison oak or poison ivy rash. These desert lovers are annual wildflowers. The species crenulata is responsible for most of the rashes found in the Southern California desert, Nevada, Arizona, Utah and New Mexico. Often the rash is around the lower leg from wandering through clumps of the plants. The rash may look the same as a poison oak or poison ivy rash, but the allergenic chemical is different and degrades when the plant dies at the end of the season.

English ivy: The stalks, leaves and roots of this common climber contain an irritant and a sensitizer that can create an allergic reaction in susceptible people that mimics the rash of poison oak and poison ivy.

Scabies: A microscopic mite burrows just under your skin causing a small red patch that can lengthen as the mite tunnels The allergic reaction resembles a poison oak or poison ivy rash. Babies then emerge on the surface of your skin and hitch a ride on anyone you hug, or dive down into your skin again. I became home to a small colony of scabies once and the little dickens had me convinced I had a mild case of poison oak. The rash spreads when the population expands.

Hives: Hives are an immediate type of an allergic reaction. The tops of the bumps are somewhat flattened. They can erupt within a matter of minutes. You feel them coming on—and they can be gone within hours after moving around the skin like puffy clouds.

Reaction from jewelry, perfume, clothing or body-care products: The rash can last for months in the same spot until you discover what causes the red, itchy, scaly or oily dermatitis and stop wearing or using it.

Ringworm: This fungal infection causes a ring of itchy red skin anywhere on your body about the size of a quarter. The outside of the ring is red and scaly.

Psoriasis: Although psoriasis itches, it has thick silvery scales with a distinct border. Knees, elbows and the scalp are common areas for this rash.

Eczema: This itchy red rash is closely related to allergies, but the exact cause is not known. Individuals with the problem are used to its many outbreaks.

Athlete's foot: This is a fungal infection. The red areas between your toes might cause you to suspect poison oak or poison ivy if you had been going barefooted.

Heat rash (prickly heat): Many people are susceptible to this itchy red rash that leaves little red pimples or welts, and they recognize it easily. Heat, tight clothes and dampness caused by sweating are the culprits.

Chiggers: You can barely see these mite larvae that insert their feeding structure into your pores or hair follicles, inject powerful digestive enzymes, and suck up the newly dead tissue (oh good lord). The small reddish welts with a hardened white center are said to itch ferociously. Chiggers are not found in the western third of the U.S.

Hot tub rash: Hot tubs, and sometimes swimming pools, can cause an infection of the skin if they are contaminated with the bacteria *pseudomonas aeruginosa*. One to two days after exposure, the skin begins to itch. Bumps form, which then change to tender red nodules that may contain pus.

Fleabites: The little buggers usually hop onto your ankles and chow down. Each bite causes a small red spot.

Pityriasis rosea: Generally harmless, this rash appears on the chest and abdomen. It begins with a small painless spot and expands to many other patches of scaly reddish-pink skin. There is a 50 percent chance of mild itching. The cause is unknown.

Dermatitis herpetiformis: Red bumps and blisters itch intensely, but also sting and burn. The rash affects arms, legs, back and buttocks. The cause is thought to be an allergy to gluten, causing celiac disease. Gastrointestinal symptoms also would occur.

HOW THE IMMUNE SYSTEM CREATES A RASH

A poison oak or poison ivy rash is the result something seemingly out of control. We frolic in the woods and later there is a slight itch. No problem, but soon the train-to-hell is on full throttle. We observe and feel the changes to our skin but, like underwater life in the ocean, the busy behind-the-scenes action is not perceived unless you don your snorkel, paddle out, and dip your face in the water. In this case, scientists have looked at the battle below the surface of the skin.

Your body is a big-time chemistry lab. It can whip up a potion that in its own right will surpass any witches' brew. The first time you are exposed to poison oak or poison ivy, you can do a full face-plant and you will have no reaction on the surface of your skin. But below, the lab is probably running full steam, creating "sensitization" in about six days.

William Epstein was one of the predominate researchers of poison oak and poison ivy. He published a study in 1986 and concluded the following:

15 to 25% are totally immune or are unlikely to be exposed to enough of the allergenic oil in their lifetime to stimulate a reaction.

25% are slightly sensitive.

25 to 50% are moderately sensitive.

10 to 25% are so exquisitely sensitive that one leaf can cause a very extreme rash.[18]

Researcher Albert Kligman wrote in 1957, "Several patients who considered themselves immune were dispossessed of this belief when I vigorously rubbed leaves on their skin. Their sensitivity was low, but definite." I love the doctor's enthusiasm, but I'm sure his patients were a bit irritated with their new rashes.[11]

This will be a bit dry here (although greatly simplified). Hopefully the stoic among you will hold on.

What is the process that causes an allergy to poison oak and poison ivy (allergic contact dermatitis)?

This is a variant of the typical Type IV hypersensitivity (discussed earlier) in that the action takes place in the top layer of skin, the epidermis, rather than lower down.

Whether you develop an allergy after the first, fifth or twenty-fifth exposure depends upon genetics. You have a threshold, and when you cross it—boom! (Unless your genetics are such that you will never react). For this tutorial, let's assume you develop an allergy after your first exposure.

First exposure to the allergenic oil

1. Within a few minutes of your first exposure, the oil (urushiol) easily begins to penetrate the epidermis by dissolving into lipids on the surface of the skin and lipids packed between cells. It moves right through the top two epidermal layers. Contact allergens (in this case, urushiol) mostly are very small molecules, fewer than 500 Daltons, that speed up movement between cells. The urushiol molecules are not yet changed, but are now called *haptens*.

2. The urushiol molecules (haptens) have reached the third layer of the epidermis (the third layer of the *first* layer of skin). For the immune system to react, the harmless molecule must first be altered.

3. Langerhans cells in this skin layer have the capability to bind small molecular compounds to their surfaces and digest the protein, thereby converting them to *antigens* (perceived as the enemy). Other cells on guard have alerted the Langerhans cells by releasing chemicals when they sensed the hapten. Now, perfectly innocent urushiol molecules have become blobs, and simply washing your skin is useless.[19]

4. The Langerhans cells display the antigen blobs on their surface.

5. T cells (T lymphocytes) migrate through the skin checking Langerhans cells, to see what they have to offer. The Langerhans cells also migrate to lymph nodes in the area, interact with T cells and present the new antigens to any T cell that genetically already has receptors complementary to this particular antigen. The T cells are unable to recognize antigens directly and need an appropriate presentation on a "silver plate," so to speak.[14]

6. The T cells proliferate. After seven to ten days there will be a colony of identical T cells capable of responding to the antigen that urushiol has become. You are now—drum roll—*allergic*. The cloned T cell descendants will diligently patrol the immune system. On your next exposure it's very likely you will have an unfortunate chain of events, culminating in allergic contact dermatitis—basically, a rash.[20]

What is the chemistry in my skin when I am *already* allergic and am exposed?

This reaction does not involve antibodies. Instead, various types of white blood cells are activated, beginning with thymic white blood cells (T cells), and later recruiting eosinophils, macrophages, neutrophils and other white blood cells into the skin.

1. As the urushiol penetrates the surface of the skin, Langerhans

cells bind to the molecules as they did during the first exposure, package them up, and present them to any T lymphocytes that are now specifically programmed to respond to the allergen—in effect, restimulating memory. The red flag goes up. More programmed T cells rush to the area, reproduce and release chemicals that orchestrate the inflammatory reaction.

2. Complicated chemistry is going on right now, causing inflammation, itching and general havoc. Among other white blood cells, eosinophils are received into the skin by the T cells and release bleach-like chemicals that irritate and inflame the skin and nerves. Histamine also joins the fray. Clear plasma from your blood seeps through vessel walls that have been rendered permeable by the chemicals. Blisters form with coverings that are parchment thin and soon tear—creating a goopy mess on the surface of your skin.

3. Macrophages (a type of white blood cell) come rushing in, adding to the carnage. Large soldiers, they release chemicals (enzymes and proteins that act as mediators of inflammation) while they tear apart the so-called enemy. They then clean the area by gobbling up the leftover garbage.

4. The battlefield is not pretty. Intense itching overpowers everything.[19, 20, 21, 22. Covers the last five paragraphs.]

HOW THE IMMUNE SYSTEM *STOPS* A RASH

Effector and Regulatory Systems

After you have experienced a number of rashes from poison oak or poison ivy, you might notice you are becoming less sensitive or, dang it, even more sensitive—apparently at whim. Encouraged by what is called our body's "effector system," inflammatory chemicals could be spewed out indefinitely, creating your own private little hell.

Something needs to stop the battle and…here it is (sound of French horns): the "regulatory system" (once called the "suppressor system"). In the middle of the pileup, specialized T cells come roaring up and put the brakes on the carnage by spewing out chemicals to subdue the bonfire—insuring that your rash will come to an end.[9, 19, 23]

The balance between the effector and regulatory systems determines the state of your allergic reaction; whichever one has the upper hand at the time calls the shots. The regulatory T cells are even capable of creating long-lasting immune tolerance, sometimes out of the blue and sometimes from long-term exposure to the allergenic oil. Attempting to control the number of regulatory T cells is the challenge many researchers are diligently working on.[9]

Immunologists would love to learn the secret to putting the regulatory system in the driver's seat. For over thirty years it has been known that several types of T cells are the central components of the regulatory system. The regulatory T cells are themselves regulated by other substances secreted by various cells of the immune system.[23, 24]

References

1. "Skin Biology and Structure." 2010. My Dr. for a Healthy Australia. wwwmydr.com.

2. "The Integument-Structure and Function." 2003. Lecture 29. www.med-ed,virginia.edu.

3. MacNeal, Robert J. 2006. "Structure and Function." www.merck.com.

4. Guin, Jere D. 2006. "Reaction Time in Experimental Poison Ivy Dermatitis. *Contact Dermatitis* 6(4):289-290.

5. Williams, J.V., J. Light and J.G. Maris, Jr. 1999. "Individual Variations in Allergic Contact Dermatitis from Urushiol." *Arch. Dermatol* 135(8).

6. McNair, James B. 1923. *Rhus Dermatitis*. The University of Chicago Press.

7. Kligman, Albert M. 1957. "Poison Ivy (Rhus) Dermatitis: An Experimental Study." Ar-

chives of Dermatology 77(2):149-180.

8. White, James Clark. 1887. *Dermatitis Venenata.*

9. Rietschel, Robert L. 2008. *Fisher's Contact Dermatitis.* BC Decker, Inc.

10. Epstein, W. L., C. R. Dawson, and R. G. Khurana. 1982. "Induction of Antigen Specific Hyposensitization to Poison Oak in Sensitized Adults." *Arch. Dermatol,* vol. 118.

11. Kligman, Albert. 1958. "Hyposensitization against Rhus dermatitis." *AMA Arch Derm* 78(1):47-72.

12. Yosipovitch, Gil, Katharing Fast, and Jeffrey D. Bernhard. 2005. "Noxious Heat and Scratching Decrease Histamine-Induced Itch and Skin Blood Flow." J. Invest. Dermatol. 125:1268-1272.

13. Baer, Harold. 1986. "Chemistry and Immunochemistry of Poisonous *Anacardiaceae.*" *Clinics in Dermatology* 4(2):152-159.

14. Kerwin, Edward M., MD. Allergist. 2010. Interview. Oregon.

15. Rytand, David A. 1948. "Fatal Anuria, the Nephrotic Syndrome and Glomerular Nephritis as Sequels of the Dermatitis of Poison Oak." *Amer. Journal of Medicine.*

16. Shaffer, Bertram, Carrol F. Burgoon, and James H. Gosman. 1951. "Acute Glomerulonephritis Following Administration of Rhus Toxin." *JAMA* 146(17):1570-1572.

17. Williford, Phillip M., and Elizabeth F. Sherertz. 1994. "Poison Ivy Dermatitis." *Arch. Fam. Med.*, vol. 3.

18. Epstein, William L. "Occupational Poison Ivy and Oak Dermatitis." *Dermatologic Clinics* 12(3):511-516.

19. Stoitzner, P., M. Zanella, U. Ortner, M. Lukas, A. Tagwerker, K. Janke, M. B. Lutz, G. Schuler, B. Echtenacher, B. Ryffel, F. Koch, and N. Romani. 1999. "Migration of Langerhans cells and dermal dendrite cells in skin organ cultures." *Journal of Leukocyte Biology,* vol. 66.

20. Kalish, Richard S., and Karyn L. Johnson. 1990. "Enrichment and Function of Urushiol (Poison Ivy)—Specific T Lymphocytes in Lesions of Allergic Contact Dermatitis to Urushiol." *Journal of Immunology* 145:3706-3713.

21. Sompayrac, Lauren. 2008. *How The Immune System Works.* Blackwell Pub., MA.

22. Kalish, Richard S. 1991. "Recent Developments in the Pathogenesis of Allergic Contact Dermatitis." *Arch. Dermatol,* vol. 127.

23. Taams, Leonie S., Arne N. Akbar and Marcan H.M. Wauben (Editors). 2005. *Regulatory T Cells in Inflammation.* Birkhäuser Verlag, MA.

24. Cavani, A, C. Albanesi, C. Traidl, S. Sebastiani, and G. Girolomoni. 2001. "Effector and Regulatory T Cells in Allergic Contact Dermatitis." *Trends in Immunology* 22(3).

The new wardrobe was a
hit—but not for long.

Chapter 9

BECOMING NONALLERGIC— CAN IT HAPPEN?

HEROIC ATTEMPTS AT DECREASING SENSITIVITY

Have some questions? Waiting with bated breath for clear, concise, condensed, cleanly packaged answers? Sorry. But you can still ask.

Is it possible to lose or lessen the allergy—to become desensitized? No. Yes. Maybe. Sometimes. Temporarily. It depends.

How long will it take? Two weeks. Six months. One year. Who knows? It depends.

How long will the desensitivity last? Three weeks. All summer. Two years. Forever. It depends.

Researchers have been flummoxed for quite awhile about the above questions.

Biologist David Senchina summed up progress in 2006. *"Hyposensitization programs in humans have been for the most part disappointing...Still, these studies demonstrate hyposensitization is possible, repeatable, and potentially effectual under the right circumstances."*[1]

I will summarize the long search for a product to desensitize folks who are allergic to poison oak and poison ivy.

The loss or reduction of an allergy goes by many names.

Tolerance: A lack of an allergy from never being exposed to the allergen, or having never developed an allergy from exposure.

Desensitivity, hardening, hyposensitivity, decreased sensitivity, hyporeactivity: For various reasons, an individual's allergy has decreased in strength.

Researcher Harold Baer wrote in 1986, *"Administering sensitizing substances to a sensitized individual is...not without hazard. Consequently, desensitization is difficult."* [2]

Serious clinical attempts to develop resistance to poison ivy in volunteers were conducted between 1919 and 1984. There were around forty-six separate studies, ranging from only four subjects on up to five hundred. The modes of exposure to the allergenic oil were oral, dermal (skin) and injection. Most studies were considered a success. Volunteers usually became partially or totally desensitized to poison ivy, but the side effects were itchy rashes during the process, which often lasted months. [3]

You may wonder how they dug up so many volunteers willing to go through what usually turned out to be a very uncomfortable experience. Well, most of the first subjects were prisoners. The warden's conversation was probably brief: "This nice doctor needs volunteers. Sign up and your sentence will be shortened, heh heh." Then there were the infants, children and adults in institutions for the severely mentally disabled who were passive subjects until laws specified otherwise. Members of the armed forces also make good subjects; they are all in one place and soldiers are trained not to whine.

In 1952, Harold Bauer voiced the accepted clinical concept of developing desensitization. *"When contact sensitivity exists, the chemical may be used to desensitize."* [2] (Pollen shots for hay fever, for example.)

In the late 1950s, after surveying the literature, Elmer Gross concluded it was difficult to evaluate the practicality of the studies. There were too many variables as to the source of the antigen (leaf, stem, fresh, dried, synthetic, etc.); the vehicle (water, alcohol, etc.);

the method of administration (oral, injection, etc.); initial concentration of the antigen; and dosage amounts. The outcome depended to a large extent upon the dosage: too small, it didn't work; too large and the side effects were unacceptable.[4]

After a 1958 study wherein volunteers became hyposensitized (still allergic, but with various degrees of reduced reaction) to poison ivy, Dr. Kligman followed the individuals for eight or nine more months. Without maintenance doses, their sensitivity slowly returned. But on the positive side, there usually were fewer allergic reactions encountered than before the study. Kligman wrote, *"The practical implications are obvious; hyposensitization must be repeated each season, or a maintenance dose has to be given perennially. A daily maintenance dose is probably advisable during the early months of summer."*[5]

Respected poison oak researcher William Epstein conducted five studies from 1974 to 1982. He reported significant hyposensitization to poison oak urushiol (the allergenic oil) with slowly escalating oral doses. Uncomfortable side effects still existed during the three- to six-month study times. Nonetheless, Dr. Epstein's upbeat conclusion in 1982 was, *"Our findings indicate that adults sensitive to poison oak/ivy can be hyposensitized by oral injections of urushiol."*[6]

Sadly, hyposensitization began fading within three months or so after the last dose was administered. Dr. Epstein hoped for future studies regarding maintenance doses, but funding was lacking.[6]

Short-lived commercial products

As various clinical studies became noticed, nine commercial products containing the allergenic oil of poison oak or poison ivy were marketed. Two were named Ivyol and Aqua Ivy.[3] I corresponded with a man who remembers as a child receiving the allergen from his doctor. He promptly broke out in a serious rash covering almost his entire body. The FDA soon decided the side effects from the products were unacceptable and revoked licensure in 1986.

My allergist set up his practice in southern Oregon in 1990. He remembers patients asking for the "poison oak shots." Those shots are still mentioned on Internet poison oak and poison ivy discussion sites with either reverence or horror.

Attempt to abolish itchy side effects in new studies

Faced with uncomfortable side effects from introducing the allergenic oil to volunteers, and with the same problem in the (soon-to-be-illegal) commercial products, researchers tried altering the chemistry of the allergenic oil so the immune system would accept it without reacting and then develop resistance to the *real* stuff.

In the mid 1980s, Dr William Epstein and associate Dr. Vera Byers attempted to create a modified form of the allergenic oil that would not only fail to induce an allergic reaction as it absorbed into the skin, but also would induce desensitization. Dr. Byers said their FDA-sanctioned supply of urushiol ran out as they were preparing for human testing and they were unable to find a standardized source. With ethics laws tightening up, the FDA became finicky and it wasn't as easy to do the clinical work anymore.[7]

There's hope

In 1984, Dr. Mahmoud ElSohly and his associates, while studying the allergenic oil of poison ivy (urushiol), developed and patented a "masked" urushiol compound designed to fool the immune system. After being injected intramuscularly, the substance enters the bloodstream, bypassing the first pass through the liver. In the circulating blood the chemical disguise is stripped away, leaving the original allergenic urushiol to bind to blood cells. At this point the immune system obligingly reacts to the urushiol by creating desensitivity *instead* of continuing with an allergic condition.[8]

Unfortunately, after an auspicious start the project never got off the ground because the company that licensed the product insisted on producing an oral preparation against Dr. ElSohly's advice. All these years later, Dr. ElSohly has started over, slightly changing his original formula—and is determined to make it all the way to market in the near future. It's looking favorable, because the product is licensed, and a company is working on development. According to

Dr. ElSohly, a physician will inject the pharmaceutical intramuscularly. One shot should create desensitivity to poison oak and poison ivy, including their close relatives, for at least six months. The actual immune chemistry as to why this happens is not yet clear, although the regulatory arm (once called "suppressor") of the immune system is suspected as playing a part.[9]

When the product finally arrives on the market, hopefully it will be announced publicly with appropriate fanfare.

The possibility of lifelong tolerance from infancy

In 1931, H. W. Straus placed poison ivy patches on the skin of newborn infants. Approximately two-thirds became sensitized. In his second study, he introduced the antigen by *mouth*. Only one-tenth became sensitized. The rest were not allergic, and never became so as long as they were studied.[10] Apparently, if the first part of the immune system in the skin (Langerhans cells) is bypassed, it might be the ticket to lifelong tolerance in those who have not yet been exposed to the antigen.[11]

The 2008 book, *Fisher's Contact Dermatitis*, briefly discusses this same phenomenon. ***"...first exposure to contact allergens by the systemic route (oral or injection for example, as opposed to skin) usually favors the development of partial or complete specific tolerance."*** [11]

This concept never took off though. Who would be the first to tell American mothers to add diced poison ivy leaves to their baby's mashed banana. Even so, researcher Kenneth Lampe wrote in 1986 regarding mango tolerance, ***"The eating of mango in infancy and continuously thereafter may result in desensitization."*** [12]

Developing desensitization at work

Researchers had been noticing something that J.D. Guin wrote about in 2001. ***"Interestingly, people who are exposed daily in their workplace tend to develop a form of individual tolerance they call hardening."*** [13]

Similarly, at the conclusion of an oft-quoted study of eight Japanese students learning the art of lacquerware (painting with an allergenic substance almost identical to poison oak and poison ivy oil), the authors wrote, "Hyposensitization to urushiol occurred among Japanese lacquer craftsmen as a result of repeated exposure to lacquer." [14]

Japanese lacquer painters are known to periodically eat a bit of allergenic lacquer paint, especially while on vacation. [15, 16, 17] I spoke to a young Japanese immigrant who remembered his parents spreading the substance on his skin to maintain his desensitization to the many lacquered products in a Japanese household. Not all are properly dried before market and may still be allergenic.

Cashew

The allergenic oil in the cashew shell (the oil of the nut itself is not allergenic) cross-reacts with poison oak and poison ivy. If you lose your sensitivity to one, you will lose sensitivity to the other. Albert Kligman found this interesting, and in 1958 attempted to create hyposensitization to poison ivy by giving volunteers cashew shell oil to ingest on their own each day. The number of drops depended on whether side effects occurred. At the conclusion of the study, Dr Kligman wrote, *"Hyposensitization [to poison ivy] may be satisfactorily achieved by the graduated oral administration of 10% cashew nut shell oil in ethyl alcohol."* He all too casually mentioned, "Skin rashes and stomatitis are the only important side-reactions." [18]

A study in 1988 came to the same conclusion as Dr. Kligman. "We have shown that hyposensitization to poison ivy occurred in the study subjects after exposure to cashew nut shell oil." [19]

Mango

Mango is another plant that cross-reacts with poison oak and poison ivy. The allergenic oil is mainly in the skin of the fruit. In Hawaii it seems locals have no problems, but when American tourists eat mangos without peeling them, they often develop a rash—usually around the mouth. An acquaintance knows a woman who ate a dish that contained mango and developed a very serious rash. For someone exceedingly allergic to poison oak or poison ivy, even the lower strength of the allergenic oil in a mango can be disastrous.

In a 2004 report, thirty-two young Americans from northern California, all allergic to poison oak, were picking mangos on a kibbutz in Israel and all broke out in a rash. Not one of the thirty local Israeli youths picking in the same orchard had an outbreak.[20]

Phillip M. Williford and associates wrote in 1994 as they were discussing the mango, *"Relative tolerance to mango dermatitis may represent a naturally occurring experiment in induction of tolerance."* [21]

Eating a leaf

Many books, articles and some herbalists casually mention that to become desensitized to poison oak and ivy, simply eat a leaf. When you brush against a leaflet you get an itsy-bitsy amount of oil on your skin—can you imagine the huge difference in quantity you would be introducing into your body by eating a whole leaflet? The ride might turn wild, and there is no getting off until the end. Two people shared with me that their experience from eating a leaf was not pleasant.

Author Euell Gibbons is often mentioned in articles on poison oak and poison ivy as the naturalist author who trumpeted the idea of dining on poison ivy leaves each spring. Not exactly. He was given instructions by an acquaintance to eat three tiny leaflets each day for three days. Do the same next week and the week after. Euell tried this technique for only two seasons before he wrote about it in his book. What nobody remembers is that he also wrote *"The effects of poison ivy vary so from person to person that I don't feel this remedy can safely be recommended for general use until further experiments are made."* [22] This particular "recipe" is fraught with danger because three spring leaflets, no matter how tiny, contain a huge amount of allergen. Repeating that amount for three days in a row would inundate the immune system with the recipe for fireworks on your skin.

Homeopathic dilution of poison ivy

Homeopathic remedies are so highly diluted, it is impossible to detect a plant molecule—yet the immune system apparently notices and responds. In the late 1930s, pharmacist Lewis Miller formulated a liquid homeopathic formula (using what he considered the optimum dilution and dosage through trial and error) made from poison ivy leaves, to be taken for seven to ten days before exposure—*the intent being to develop a resistance to poison oak and poison ivy*. The dose can continue to be taken each day for as long as resistance is needed. Plant molecules are not pharmaceutically detectable; therefore, it is considered safe and allowed on the market.

This use of a homeopathic preparation as a preventative medication was quite groundbreaking—these preparations are traditionally used for treatment of symptoms.

Miller's son Robert said in an interview, ***"Dad's theory on this was if you take frequent micro-doses of something, it will help you build up a resistance."***[23]

From 1953 to 1957, Dr. Elmer Gross agreed to conduct four separate clinical studies on Miller's product. He used a total of four hundred and fifty-five volunteers who were allergic to poison ivy. The result of all four studies was, ***"76% of the subjects were either free of ivy dermatitis or experienced milder attacks."***[4] (See the commercial products section at the back of the book).

Goat milk

Why does everybody keep asking if you can lessen your allergy to poison oak and poison ivy by drinking milk from goats that ate the plants? Do they think goat keepers regularly feed their animals armloads of poison ivy? I certainly never did. A carefully designed study proved that the allergenic substance would *not* end up in the milk anyway, so that's that! The study showed that goat *pellets* would contain the allergenic oil, but nobody's talking about eating *them*.[24]

Honey and pollen

Poison oak and poison ivy flowers, of course, produce nectar and pollen—neither of which contains the allergenic oil because it is formed in the resin canals of the plant tissue. Enjoy your tea with honey, but you are *not* losing your allergy.

Summing up, Dr Kligman felt, after concluding a number of studies, that complete clinical desensitization to poison oak and poison ivy can be achieved, *but not in a highly sensitive subject*. The same conclusion was reached by a group of researchers in 1998 when experimenting on guinea pigs. They wrote, *"The intensity of sensitization is a factor related to the difficulty in inducing hyposensitization."* [16] Kligman also noted that hyposensitization is temporary and begins to wane after awhile. He noted that the original sensitivity to the plants returns within six to ten months or longer *if the antigen is not reintroduced periodically*.[5]

In 1990 a group of researchers introduced blood serum from resistant human subjects to mice with an allergy to poison oak and poison ivy. The mice then became resistant. A little parlor trick.[25]

Other immune conditions

We have been discussing poison oak and poison ivy tolerance, but there is a whole range of medical conditions involving similar immune system disorders that researchers have valiantly been working on. J.D. Issacs wrote in 2007, "The concept and practice of therapeutic tolerance has successfully been applied to animal models of autoimmunity…for more than two decades. Finally there are encouraging signs of its translation to clinical practice."[26]

"Immune tolerance is the Holy Grail of immunology."
Dr. Anthony Gaspari 2008[27]

References

1. Senchina, David S. 2006. "Ethnobotany of Poison Ivy, Poison Oak and Relatives (Toxicodendron spp., Anacardiaceae) in America: Veracity of Historical Accounts." *Rhodora* 108(935):203-227.

2. Baer, Harold. 1986. "Chemistry and Immunochemistry of Poisonous Anacardiaceae." *Clinics in Dermatology* 4(2):152-159.

3. Watson, Sue E. 1986. "Toxicodendron Hyposensitization Programs." *Clinics in Dermatology* Apr-June 4(2):160-170.

4. Gross, Elmer. 1958. "An Oral Antigen Preparation in the Prevention of Poison Ivy Dermatitis: Results in 455 Cases of Ivy Sensitivity." *Industrial Medicine and Surgery* 273:142-144.

5. Kligman, Albert. 1958. "Hyposensitization against Rhus dermatitis." *AMA Arch Derm* 78(1):47-72.

6. Epstein, W. L., C. R. Dawson, and R. G. Khurana. 1982. "Induction of Antigen Specific Hyposensitization to Poison Oak in Sensitized Adults." *Arch. Dermatol*, vol. 118.

7. Byers, Vera. 2010. Allergist-Immunologist. Phone interview.

8. Vietmeyer, Noel. 1986. "Science Has Got its Hands on Poison Ivy, Poison Oak, and Poison Sumac." *US Dept. of Agriculture Fire Management Notes* 47(1).

9. ElSohly Mahmud. 2010. Research Professor, Research Institute of Pharmaeutical Sciences. University of Mississippi. Phone interview.

10. Straus, H.W. 1934. "Experimental Study of the Etiology of Dermatitis Venenata. Journal of Allervy 5(6):588-570.

11. Rietschel, Robert L. 2008. *Fisher's Contact Dermatitis*. BC Decker, Inc

12. Lampe, Kenneth D. 1986. *"Dermatitis-Producing Anacardiaceae of the Carribbean Area." Cl. in Derm.* 4(2):179-182.

13. Guin, Jere D. 2001. "Treatment of Toxicodendron Dermatitis (Poison Ivy and Poison Oak)." *Skin Therapy Letter* 6(7):3-5.

14. Kayai, Kehchi. 1991. "Hyposensitization to Urushiol among Japanese Lacquer Craftsmen." *Contact Dermatitis* 25(5): 290-295.

15. Nelson, Lewis S., Michael Balick and Nieve Shere. 2008. "What Is This Plant and Why Is This Japanese Artist Eating It?" *Journal of Medical Toxicology* 4(3):201-202.

16. Crawford, Glen. 2009. "Botanical Dermatology." www.emedicine.medscape.com.

17. Ikeda, Y., H. Yasuno, A. Sato, and K. Kawai. 1998. "Oral and Epicutaneous Desensitization in Urushiol Contact Dermatitis in Guinea Pigs Sensitized by Two Methods of Different Sensitizing Potency." *Contact Dermatitis* 39:286-292.

18. Kligman, Albert M. 1958. "Cashew Nut Shell Oil for Hyposensitization against Rhus Dermatitis." *AMA Arch Derm* 78(3).

19. Reginella, Ruthane F., James C. Fairfield, and James G. Marks, Jr. 1989. "Hyposensitization to Poison Ivy after Working in a Cashew Nut Shell Oil Processing Factory." *Contact Dermatitis* 20(4):274-279.

20. Hershko, K., I. Weinberg, and A. Ingber. 2005. "Exploring the Mango-Poison Ivy Connection: The Riddle of Discriminative Plant Dermatitis." *Contact Dermatitis* 52(1):3-5.

21. Williford, Phillip M., and Elizabeth F. Sherertz. 1994. "Poison Ivy Dermatitis." *Arch. Fam. Med.*, vol. 3.

22. Gibbons, Euell. 1962. *Stalking the Wild Asparagus.* David McKay Co., NY.

23. Ruff, Kathy. 2005. "Homeopathic Remedy for Poison Ivy has Eastern Pa. Roots." *Eastern Pennsylvania Business Journal* May 30-June 5.

24. Straus, H.W. 1934. "Experimental Study of the Etiology of Dermatitis Venenata. Journal of Allervy 5(6):588-570.

25. Stampf, J.L., N. Castagnoli, W. Epstein, R.W. Baldwin, and V. Byers. 1990. "Suppression of Urushiol-Induced Delayed-Type Hypersensitivity Responses in Mice with Serum IgG Immunoglobulin from Human Hyposensitized Donors." *J. of Invest. Derm.* 95(3):363-365.

26. Isaacs, J.D. 2007. "T Cell Immunomodulation—the Holy Grail of Therapeutic Tolerance." *Curr. Opin. Pharmacol* 7(4):418-425.

27. Franklin, Deborah. 2008. "Pill to Prevent Poison Ivy Itch Proves Elusive." National Public Radio. www.npr.org.

Dressed for the kill.

Chapter 10

PREVENTIVE MEASURES

BLOCKING ALLERGENIC OIL FROM YOUR SKIN

Sounds great: apply a product, frolic among poison ivy plants—no worries. Ah, if everything in life was this simple. Blink, blink. Now back to reality. There are barrier products, and at least one even does a very good job, but there's the problem of sweat, getting wet, missing spots when applying, removing clothing or rolling up sleeves and dang—leaving the bottle home.

Commercial product

There are a few blocking products on the market. I found one that has been clinically tested and the results made public. The active ingredient is organoclay, a chemical alteration of bentonite clay that greatly increases its oil absorbing power. Poison oak researcher William Epstein worked with a lab formulating the product in the 1980s. An oil block is a godsend for extremely allergic individuals. If not perfect, it gives them a greater chance to make it through a hike unscathed. (See "Commercial Products.")

Clay

Drat, your shortcut is taking you through a huge patch of poison ivy. Don't fret—you can make your own oil block in the field, but it's a bit messy. Slather mud all over exposed areas. For a less effective (but quick) block, dig down for dirt under leaves and such, and rub it over your skin. If you brought bentonite clay with you, better yet. When in the clear, rub the dirt off with a cloth. Find more dry dirt and rub all over your skin in a scrubbing motion to absorb and rub off any lingering oil.

A post on an Internet discussion site suggested buying a men's deodorant with talc (an absorbent). Well, I did. The liquid glaze wouldn't dry, application was patchwork and I smelled as though I were really worried about underarm odor.

WASHING THE ALLERGENIC OIL OFF YOUR SKIN

Here it is: one of the most important chapters in the book. I would love to give you a fighting chance and tell you in three easy steps how to remove poison oak or poison ivy oil from your skin. *But—* and I dither here—everyone seems to have an opinion, although nobody really knows firsthand, because there doesn't seem to *be* a firsthand, that is, scientific, peer-reviewed studies on all options. The articles available are usually theories, guesses and rumors that have been handed down from article to article throughout the years. I guess I might as well add to the pile.

Friends tell me about washing with mild soap and never getting a rash. Others use powerful solvents and manage to break out in a head-to-toe case.

There is nothing in the world that can produce such divergent experiences as the oil urushiol. It would be nice if you could actually *see* what you are supposed to remove, or know if it's actually there. But life isn't always perfect, is it?

"This sticky substance will adhere to the skin like pitch and is as difficult to remove."[1]

Remove the allergenic oil immediately when you've been contaminated. Don't come home hours later and shower with your special product, thinking all's well.

In 1941 B. S. Shelmire did a little experiment by rubbing poison ivy leaves on his palms and washing well five minutes later. Supposedly his hands were perfectly clean, yet he managed to cause contact dermatitis on six individuals.[2] When your hands become contaminated with the oil, they are now loaded weapons. If they are *heavily* contaminated, they could be called "weapons of mass destruction."

Dr. Kligman continued the "hand-as-weapon" experiment in 1957. He rubbed fresh resin from poison ivy leaves on the thumb of a nonallergic volunteer. The thumb was then pressed against the back of another nonallergic volunteer four hundred and ninety-nine times. The last thumb press was against the skin of a courageous, highly allergic volunteer, who developed a rash (thankfully mild)—proving the thumb was still "loaded."[3]

The "window of opportunity"

The ever-enthusiastic Dr. Kligman conducted a study to determine how soon the oil needed to be removed from the skin to completely *prevent* a rash. The conclusion: within five minutes for the highly sensitive, and under thirty minutes for the mildly sensitive. As you can see, the highly sensitive need to be on the alert, whereas the mildly sensitive can afford to be a bit sloppy in cleanup.[3] There was a study in 2000 that demonstrated that the oil *does* begin to penetrate the skin quickly, but not all at once. By removing the oil remaining on the surface, even as long as two hours after exposure, the immune system has less to react to in the long term. That person will develop a milder rash than the individual whose arm was never washed, unless, of course, one of them has a much higher degree of sensitivity than the other.[4]

You can contaminate others regardless of whether you are allergic yourself. Dr Kligman rubbed poison ivy leaves on the backs of two nonsensitive volunteers and covered the spots. Three days later, the dressings were removed. A thumb was pressed against the contaminated backs and then on the skin of sensitive subjects. The rashes that developed proved that, even after three days, not all of the oil had been absorbed by the skin.[3]

Okay, let's get down to the nitty-gritty. You can mix and match your urushiol removers. If one doesn't work, maybe the other will. Heck, the stuff is invisible—shoot all six barrels.

Water degrading the oil

There is a widely accepted theory, passed down from noted poison oak researcher William Epstein (I heard it from him in 1978), that water "degrades" urushiol, the allergenic oil in the resin of the plants. So if you are exposed, wash with plain water. I could find no studies concerning this technique, plus two of his colleagues informed me they heartily disagreed. Moisture *is* needed to oxidize urushiol into a hard nonallergenic state, but rather than degrade the oil, water would stimulate the oxidation process, which assisted by the enzyme laccase, could take hours to months depending on moisture and warmth. By then, of course, the urushiol would have been absorbed into the skin.

Clay

Free earth

Get down on your hands and knees. No need to pray, just push leaf litter aside to expose the real earth, the CLAY. Guess what? Clay absorbs oil. Ever been outside and someone spilled car oil on the concrete driveway? If they were smart, they dumped a shovel full of dirt over the oil and let it absorb the goop.

Same concept applies for poison oak or poison ivy oil. Scoop up big handfuls of dry clay and scrub like mad. The grit will help dislodge the oil. If it's damp or wet, you will need to let it dry on your skin to free up room for more absorption, but you will lose time waiting. It's very important you don't scrub with composted leaves, so put some energy into moving organic matter aside.

Commercial earth: Bentonite clay

This is the type of clay I use. It has huge absorbent abilities, being able to expand up to three times its volume by binding water, oil, and even bacteria to its surface. Rub dry bentonite on your skin immediately if you think you were contaminated. Oil will be pulled into the clay. Continue adding more clay as you rub. Each layer will scrape the lower layers off, then you can rub your hands together with more clay, removing all the resin and oil—hopefully.

You don't need water to do the job. You can apply clay quickly, on the run so to speak. Another nice quality is if it escapes your packaging, it's not that big of a deal. Just shake it out like dirt. Check out "Commercial Products" at the back of the book.

There are even more benefits if you bring clay along. . Put a spoonful in your water bottle to create an electrolyte drink. Give yourself a facial. Pack a cut, infection, abscess or burn with wet clay to speed healing. It must stay moist, though. No toothpaste? Brush with clay. Need a brick house...?

Hopefully you now realize that wherever you are, you can always find something with which to clean your skin. Dirt is everywhere. Dirt is good.

Grit

When you think about it, the *resin* that contains the allergenic oil should be in the picture. Pine pitch is a terpene resin, and is sticky as all get-out, but poison oak and ivy exude a phenolic resin; not as sticky as pine resin, but known to be harder to remove from the skin than plain oil.

Various grits are added to products for removing oils and resins to kind of scrape them from the skin. I like pumice (finely ground volcanic rock). It feels like fine sand. It's okay for most skin, but not your face. Oatmeal is popular in some specialty bars for poison oak and poison ivy. An oatmeal bar would be nice for your face and the gentle texture would assist in dislodging the oil. Clay is gentle enough for your face. The particles are very fine. Some of the poison oak and poison ivy bar soaps contain clay.

Certain commercial products specific for poison oak and poison ivy contain tiny plastic balls that seem to work well as grit.

Limonene

Press orange peels and you get limonene. Yes, it does have a perky orange smell. It's a powerful grease remover, a wonderful replacement for the petroleum-based mineral spirits in so many commercial products. Some of us don't care a whit; just want the job done. Other folks are very "green." Limonene will please both camps. It's packaged as an all-around household cleanser in spray bottles in natural foods stores, but I was really impressed when I saw a product in an online catalog for forest workers. It contained limonene and was designed to remove resin from power tools. Apparently, tough guys clean their huge resin-covered power tools with limonene. I was sold. If it does all that, it will surely remove poison oak and poison ivy resin, which is wimpy compared to pine pitch. It's possible to develop an allergic rash from limonene, but very few people do.

Limonene and pumice: a perfect mixture

After I teamed limonene and pumice together in my mind, I went in search for a product. I found a couple in auto supply stores, but lots of other stores carry them. You apply this stuff *without* water and wring your hands together vigorously. The pumice is not abrasive, unless you use it on your face or have delicate skin. Rinse with water, and repeat a couple of times. When dirty car oil and grease is gone, at least you can see the difference. With urushiol, no such luck. You will find out in a couple of days how the cleansing went.

Limonene is new to the tough oil and grease remover market, so the companies still market their old tried-and-true formulations filled with harsh toxic petrochemicals. You need to look for a drawing of an orange on the label. The ingredients are limonene and pumice, and not a whole lot more. The gel squeezes out from a plastic bottle. If the ingredients include mineral spirits, you have the wrong product.

Soap

How soap works

Soap traps oil in such a way that it can be washed away in water whose surface tension is flattened, allowing the water molecules to flow into smaller openings. Surfactants added to soaps are wetting agents that lower the interfacial tension between two liquids. They solubilize urushiol, the allergenic oil—if the soap is strong enough.

Liquid Soap

Liquid dishwasher soap is often mentioned on Internet discussion groups for its ability to remove allergenic oil. It certainly cleans dishes well.

Bar soap

Lye soaps are sometimes touted for strong oil-removing properties. The idea is, if it's strong, the oil has no chance. On the other hand, gentle bathroom soaps tend to smear the allergenic oil around rather than wash it off. Small companies still make traditional lye soap, but the old Fels Naphtha bar soap everyone used in the past no longer contains the petroleum product naphtha or mineral spirits. Now it's regular soap and chemicals, but the company markets it as though it never changed.

There are some interesting bar soaps these days designed for poison oak and poison ivy. They are often composed of safe, natural ingredients like herbs, clay, and oatmeal, including various types of grit, to help dislodge the sticky resin. Some of these soaps are so gentle, they help heal your skin if used during the rash episode.

Bar soaps are easy to carry around in your pack or car. They don't spill and make a mess.

Vegetable oil

For seven thousand years the Japanese have been creating lacquerware with a tree resin that includes the allergenic oil urushiol. Poison oak and poison ivy urushiol is only slightly different chemically. I figured the folks who have been exposed to the oil for a long time would have a pretty good hit on the best way to remove it. Vegetable oil was the favored product for each of the three lacquer painters I spoke with. Flax, rapeseed, and cashew nut oil were used, but they said any oil would work. Rub the oil on the skin, and the allergenic oil will dissolve into it. Remove the oil mixture with a dry cloth and wash well with a strong soap and water. One painter said she used her commercial oil-based skin cream.

Jewelweed *Impatiens aurea* (touch-me-not, snapweed)

James Duke, an authority on healing herbs, had a dramatic little demonstration for his herb workshops. He rubbed the inside of both wrists with poison ivy leaves. A minute or two later, he wiped one wrist with a ball of crushed jewelweed leaves and stems. Three days later, the wrist rubbed with jewelweed would have a minor eruption or none at all, while the untended wrist would be itchy with a poison ivy rash.[5] Jewelweed is touted for stopping the itch, but preventing the rash is even more important.

Alcohol

The allergenic oil, urushiol, easily dissolves into alcohol, but alcohol evaporates quickly and disappears, depositing the oil back on the skin. Pour alcohol on a cloth or tissue and wipe, removing the alcohol and oil together. Wash with soap and water. You can use hard liquor if this is all you have.

I met a woman who said she had a high fever as a child. She was bathed in alcohol and developed alcohol poisoning. Don't overdo it when using alcohol; it can be toxic if used over large areas.

Large, individual towelettes impregnated with alcohol or other oil-removing chemicals work well. These are easy to pop into your backpack, but costly because they can be used only once. Regular alcohol hand wipes, being small and on the dry side, are not effective.

Vinegar

The way vinegar cleans windows attests to its strength. Vinegar is safe and cheap.

Showering

Many people suggest using tepid water because hot water will thin the oil, allowing it to slide down the walls of the follicles (what are wrongly called pores). Follicles do not open *into* your body, but the oil is now in a little cave, safe from scrubbing. (Real "pores" contain sweat glands, and don't open and close.)

Don't just jump into the shower. There is too much chance of smearing the oil around unnecessarily. Carefully spot clean as much as you can. If you feel you must shower, use something strong, not the delicate soaps so often kept in bathrooms.

Bleach

Some folks rub straight bleach on their skin. If not quickly washed off, this caustic chemical can leave burn scars that will last for years. Use vinegar or rubbing alcohol instead. They are just as good.

Ammonia

For some strange reason ammonia still has its supporters. This chemical once was a fixture in every home as a strong cleanser when mixed with water. It can etch metals, and when mixed with chlorine forms a dangerous gas. Besides the above, straight ammonia can burn the skin. Ammonia is an ingredient in smelling salts, so if a delicate soul faints in fear at the sight of a poison ivy bush, waft a little under his/her nose.

Strong solvents

Turpentine: Gum turpentine is distilled from resin, and wood turpentine from the wood of the pine tree. It's okay if it's from a plant, right? No. Actually it's one of the worst. Turpentine is used as a solvent and is in many cleaning products. It is also antiseptic and has a "clean scent." It is so toxic that the U.S. Department of Labor has four pages of safety instructions for workers. Inhale too much and you stop breathing.

Kerosene: Derived from refined petroleum, kerosene is toxic and has toxic additives (principally benzene and naphtha).

Mineral spirits: Also called Stoddard solvent, this is a petroleum distillate used as paint thinner. It is less flammable and less toxic than turpentine. Odorless mineral spirits have been further refined, and some toxic compounds have been removed. Still, it's an eye and skin irritant—and harmful if inhaled.

Paint thinner: This stuff can be filled with all sorts of bad things. For example, turpentine, acetone, toluene, acetic acid, butanone, benzene, naphtha, butanol.

Gasoline: Benzene, toluene, xylene, ethanol, methanol, and methyl tertiary butyl ether. Yikes.

Deactivate the allergenic oil

There are popular products on the market that claim their chemicals penetrate the skin and deactivate urushiol, even after a day or so; and stop the rash in its tracks. Respected poison oak researcher William Epstein wrote that within four to six hours after contamination, the oil could be leached out of the skin using water mixed with an organic solvent such as acetone or alcohol.[6] This would need to happen before the oil was changed chemically by the immune system and transported into the lymph. I did not see the article myself (it is no longer available from the publisher) and have not heard of a clinical study done on this subject.

SO, WE ALL COME HOME, wash like mad to remove this invisible stuff that maybe we are smearing all over ourselves, or maybe not. We use this and that—with no way of knowing if anything we are doing is really helping. If there was a chemical we could spread over our skin that would turn the urushiol pink, now *that* would be a popular product.

WASHING YOUR CLOTHES

CLOTHING

Upon arriving home, dump your clothing and your dog in the washing machine first thing. Actually, if you just wipe your dog with a cloth soaked with alcohol, he/she won't kick up as much of a fuss. If, heaven forbid, you take a shower first, and emerge sparkling clean, pull on disposable vinyl (not latex) gloves before dealing with your clothes. Every household should have a box of gloves. Lacking these, use chopsticks to move your clothing if you have to, but do not touch the fabric.

Let's say you think your shirt is contaminated and it's a pullover. While tugging it over your head, your face and hair will be smeared with allergenic oil. The answer is simple. Put another shirt on over the one you're wearing. Pull the two off together and slam dunk both into the washing machine.

Hot water and lots of strong laundry detergent is recommended. Heat breaks up oil molecules, assisting soap to emulsify them. I like to add limonene, a nontoxic, powerful oil remover made from pressing orange peels. Natural foods stores carry these products diluted as household cleansers, but I bought the pure stuff online and now add a splash in my washing machine.

Albert Kligman, a tireless researcher in the 1950s, conducted a few experiments with clothing he rubbed with poison ivy leaves. One important conclusion was "Sap [actually resin] contaminated clothing was rendered harmless after washing in an automatic laundering machine using commercial detergent."[3]

Dr. Kligman did a little experimenting to see how the oil reacted under different humidities and temperatures. He placed contaminated clothing in a thirty-seven degree environment with one hundred percent humidity. Within three to five days, the allergenic oil had *oxidized* and was no longer allergenic. If the room had been warm, it would have oxidized sooner. Doing the opposite, he placed other contaminated clothing in a very *dry* environment (a desicator) at room temperature. After nine months the clothing was *still* allergenic. As you can see, left damp and warm, clothes, tools, etc., will lose their allergenic tendency fairly quickly, but tossed in a dry, protected area, nothing much changes. Check out the chapter that includes the "Japanese lacquer tree," wherein I explain the weird *drying* of lacquer art pieces.[3]

PLANT REMOVAL

Thinking of removing some poison oak or poison ivy from your property? First rent a backhoe with an enclosed cab—then a deep-sea diving outfit...

Are you pretty allergic to poison oak and poison ivy? You *will* get contaminated. You *will* get a rash, no matter how careful you are—even if you use every suggestion in this chapter.

The dratted stuff is *invisible*. Who knows where it landed on your body, or if you smeared it around. This chapter is for those of you who every so often develop small rashes, but in general are pretty tolerant. You could be in for a big surprise, though. Damp leaf shreds flying around from a weed whacker, mower or a branch dripping allergenic resin are a lot different from a light brush against a poison oak or poison ivy leaflet while hiking.

One fine morning, my son-in-law Chip trotted out to his poison oak jungle on his recently purchased country acreage—all suited up and shouldering a brand new super-duper weed whacker. Within two days I had a good test subject for my collection of commercial remedies I was dying to try out.

What went wrong? The mesh on the pull-down face protector of the chain-saw helmet was no match for the plant resin flying through the air at fifty miles an hour. Splat—right on his cheek. Onward ho. Pieces of leaves and stems flying around like wet green confetti later left proof on his wrists that his gloves didn't always meet his shirtsleeves. Although his hands, encased in thick canvas work gloves, stayed pure as newly fallen snow, he immediately contaminated them after the job by removing his resin-covered garments with bare hands. Unfortunately, the allergenic oil is in the resin. He then stepped into the shower and proceeded to smear poison oak oil all over his chest and behind his neck with the help of mild bath soap. Later he carefully placed his clothes into the washing machine using kitchen tongs, and settled in for the night.

Chip, undaunted by this experience, plans to change his techniques a bit, and will march back out—as soon as his rash clears up.

Hip clothing for the front line

Coveralls: Buy a pair—long-sleeved; you will be glad you did. The top and bottom are attached and it's easily removed—much safer than pulling a shirt over your head and smearing your face and hair with allergenic oil. Zippers are easier to deal with than buttons. Paint stores carry coveralls, but janitorial supply companies might have a wider variety. They are priced around sixteen dollars used, and twenty-four to thirty dollars new. Wear your coveralls over regular clothing for extra protection. The oil *can* work its way through fabric, as proven when my cousin wore the same pants two days in a row after shredded poison ivy leaves peppered his legs while mowing. The allergic reaction left his thighs a mess.

Shirts: If you have no coveralls, choose a button or zippered long-sleeved shirt. When a pullover is the only option: at job completion, don non-rubber gloves and put a clean shirt on over the contaminated one. Pull the two off together—the clean shirt will protect your face and hair. Now you see why coveralls make sense. Unzip them, let them fall from your body and delicately step away.

Rubber bands: Wear overly long sleeves and place rubber bands at the wrists. They work well to keep the sleeves in place.

Neck protection: Wear a bandana around your neck with the knot at the back and triangle in the front. Wayward branches seem to spring back toward the face or neck. If need be, pull the scarf over your nose to protect your lower face. This will give you an attractive, mysterious look.

Heavy gloves: Canvas or leather work gloves with stiff extended collars that cover the lower forearms work best for serious plant removal. Lighter duty gloves, the ones with elastic wristbands, leave gaps between the gloves and sleeves. Avoid touching your face with your gloves. Of course, your nose will itch incessantly the whole time. For a bit more protection, wear thin vinyl gloves under the heavy ones, and drop some extras in your pocket. When removing the clumsy outer gloves for any reason, your hands remain uncontaminated.

Vinyl (surgical type) gloves: Be certain you don't have latex gloves, which are made from rubber. The allergenic oil urushiol dissolves right through rubber. Vinyl gloves are excellent for jobs like pulling up small poison oak or poison ivy plants, wiping down the dog, cleaning tools and performing minor surgery.

Safety helmet with face protector: When cutting tall bushes, use a safety helmet (for chain sawing and weed whacking) with a strong screen that pulls down to cover your face. Be aware that some of the gunk might get through if you are weed whacking. A plastic face shield will protect from flying resin, but plastic scratches and fogs up. Both types, attached to helmets, are around twenty-four dollars.

Barrier product: Consider this type of product, especially for yur face. Studies show they prevent at least some of the allergenic oil from reaching your skin. (See "Commercial Products.")

Washing clothing

Wash your clothes as soon as possible, before the allergenic oil oxidizes and hardens. Don't forget your shoes and gloves.

Wear vinyl gloves, or lacking these, place plastic bags over your hands and work through them to remove your clothing. Use warm or hot water and a strong laundry detergent. I suggest adding limonene, a nontoxic, powerful oil remover made from pressing orange peels. See the chapter on removing oil from clothing for more information.

Killing or controlling the plants

Digging up: The best time to remove these plants is after the leaves have fallen and when the soil is wet. I try to cut the stems first for access to the root clump. The surface roots are actually rooted stems (rhizomes). Roots grow downward from the rhizome as the clump ages, making removal difficult in hard soil. Young plants are quite easy to dig up, but they often break apart, leaving pieces to sprout next season, so continue to turn the soil and search them out.

Small individual seedlings in a lawn or garden: I am somewhat tolerant now, so I pull them up with bare hands, then scrub my hands with dirt right there. I don't need water, because the clay sops up the oil and the grit helps to dislodge it. A handy technique is to slip your hands into plastic bags. Grasp the plant at its base through the bag, pull the plant out of the ground, and slide the bag over the plant. Your hands are protected, and the plant is packed and ready to trash.

Lawns and meadows: Some experts say repeated tillage, cutting or mowing at or near ground level will eventually kill the plants if done for several years.[7] "Repeated" is the key word here. Our meadow is mowed only two or three times in the spring and early summer. The plants never die, but they stay short—about six inches tall. Our other meadow is never cut, and is dotted with poison oak bushes. Most stay about three feet tall because of full sun and dry soil.

Tall vines: I was cutting the trunks of poison oak vines that were growing up fir trees, and pulling down the huge plants. Then I realized they were not actually a threat. The first leaves were twenty feet up the tree.

Smothering: Cut the plants close to the ground and lay old carpeting, plastic, tarps, etc., on top. Thick stacks of newspapers or cardboard might work. The question is which would give up the ghost first, the paper or the plants.

Composting: I downloaded a couple of online conversations from the Internet regarding the feasibility of small-batch and large-batch composting. At the end of long discussions and elaborate theories, the conclusion was that little is known about the break-down chemistry of the oil in a composting system. There is a good chance it would go through the process and emerge still allergenic, ready to contaminate the gardener.

Animals: Horses, sheep and cows will eat poison oak and poison ivy. Goats are considered the animal of choice if you want the plants munched down and your roses pruned. By the way, studies have shown that none of the allergenic oil finds its way into goat milk.[8]

Insects: Although many insects feed on the leaves, bark and stems of *Toxicodendrons*, two insects have been suggested for further studies: The poison ivy or argid sawfly (*Arge humeralis*, and the pyralid moth (*Epipaschia zelleri*). Insects are problematic: they are short-lived and need constant monitoring.[9]

Fungus: There are about nineteen species of fungus that negatively affect poison oak or poison ivy that might be options for future study.[9]

Any consideration of introducing insects, fungus or animals to control *Toxicodendron* growth needs thought concerning negative effects on the ecology of the area, especially if the proposed introduction is a nonnative species that might affect the area in other ways.[9]

Natural herbicides

Vinegar: There is mention on Internet discussion sites about vinegar. Use distilled white vinegar and spray on the leaves. It will take longer than chemical herbicides, but supposedly it works. If not, the vinegar was cheap.

Salt: There also are discussions on the Internet about using salt to kill plants. An environmentally sensitive landscaper cautioned against this. Salt is toxic to the soil and persistent for years. It can leach into streams and groundwater. The landscaper feels it is more damaging than using chemical herbicides.

Chemical herbicides

I dislike thinking about chemicals like herbicides. My husband and I live organically as much as possible, and once sold vegetables and flowers from our small certified organic truck farm. Hopefully you will use a safe alternative, like hiring a commercial gardener—who is not allergic—to dig up and remove the plants.

While it makes sense to cut or dig up the plants when the leaves have fallen, herbicides need to be applied during the growing season so the leaves can absorb the chemicals.

Supposedly the first sign of impending demise is curling and twisting. It might take a week or two to look dead. Resprouting may occur from areas of the root system that the chemical missed. Respray after these sprouts reach eight or ten inches. You need enough leaf area to transport the chemical downward.

The two main herbicides for the job are tricolpyr and glyphosate. At least one company includes both chemicals in its product. You need to look for the words "poison ivy" on the label to get the product specified for these plants, because the basic weed-killer formulas are not strong enough to do the job without repeated applications. This is according to a customer service representative at a company that markets Monsanto and Ortho products.

Tricolpyr and glyphosate are *systemic* herbicides, which means the poison moves inside the plants to the roots.

Because the poison ivy formulas are stronger than regular weed formulas, do not use these on lawns or near any plants or trees you don't want to kill.

Disposing of herbicide containers: Never pour an herbicide down the sink or storm drain. Herbicides are "hazardous waste" products. Partially empty containers need to be taken to a special place for disposal. Each city has its own process. Call your local recycling company.

These products are always a danger to small children who probably will not drink the foul stuff, but might spill it all over themselves.

Today's herbicides may be a safer alternative than those used in past years. In 1926 the U.S. Department of Agriculture recommended spraying poison oak and poison ivy with kerosene (distillation of petroleum), sodium arsenite solution (a salt), or treating the cut stems with sulfuric acid (corrosive).[1] That same year, James McNair, a highly regarded researcher of poison oak and poison ivy, thought nothing of recommending iron chloride, a toxic, highly corrosive and acidic compound.[10]

Burning the plants:

NEVER EVER BURN POISON OAK OR POISON IVY BRANCHES, LEAVES OR ROOTS. THE OIL DOES NOT EVAPORATE. IT WILL BE IN THE SMOKE ATTACHED TO ASHES AND SOOT. YOU WILL BE ENJOYING THE FIRE WHILE URUSHIOL IS EMERGING FROM THE FLAMES LIKE THE TERMINATOR—ONLY IT'S INVISIBLE.

References

1. "Poison Ivy." 1926. Field Museum of Natural History Leaflet 12. Dept. of Botany, Chicago.

2. Shelmire, B.S. 1941. "Hyposensitization to Poison Ivy." *Arch Dermatol Syph.* 44:983.

3. Kligman, Albert M. 1957. "Poison Ivy (Rhus) Dermatitis: An Experimental Study." Archives of Dermatology 77(2):149-180.

4. Stibich, A.S., M. Yagan, V. Sharma, B. Herndon and C. Montgomery. 2000. "Cost-Effective Post-Exposure Prevention of Poison Ivy Dermatitis." *International Journal of Dermatology* Jul;39(7):515-518.

5. Duke, James A. 1997. *The Green Pharmacy*. Rodale Press, PA.

6. Epstein, William L. 1994. "Occupational Poison Ivy and Oak Dermatitis." *Dermatologic Clinics* 12(3):511-516.

7. Czarnota, Mark. 2006. Weed Wizard: Controlling Poison Ivy in the Landscape. Univ. of

Georgia Cooperative Extension Circular 867-10.

8. Kouakou, Brou, David Rampersad, Eloy Ridriguez, and Dan L. Brown. 1992."Research Indicates Dairy Goats Used to Clear Poison Oak Do Not Transfer Toxicant to Milk." California Agriculture 46(3):4-6.

9. Senchina, David S. 2008. "Fungal and Animal Associates of Toxicodendron spp. (Anacardiaceae) in North America." *Perspectives in Plant Ecology, Evolution and Systematics* 10:197-216.

10. McNair, James B. 1923. *Rhus Dermatitis*. The University of Chicago Press.

Chapter 11

DEALING WITH THE ITCH

EXPLAINING THE ITCH PHENOMENON

It's the brain that itches, not the skin[1]

Most folks would probably choose pain over an itchy rash anytime. For one thing, you can take a pain pill, settle back and read a book. But **"There's no drug focused on itch"** according to researcher Dr. Gil Yosipovitch, the "Godfather of Itch," in 2007. When I spoke to him near the end of 2010, things were about the same.[2]

Researchers once suspected that an itch was just a small pain; now it is common knowledge that "Itch and pain are different sensations. Each is processed by distinct sets of neurons."[3] Because of the separation, pain medications, including oral anti-inflammatory over-the-counter agents like aspirin, will have no effect on your poison oak or poison ivy itch. Opiates (morphine, codeine, etc.) may even increase the itch.[3, 4]

It has been determined in the last ten years or so that there are two separate neuropathways for itch sensation. When histamine is released in an allergic reaction (like poison oak and poison ivy), it has its very own nerve fibers eager to send messages to the brain via the spinal cord—"Give it all you got." The brain complies with a returning message: "Let there be itch."[5]

Other itch-specific sets of nerve fibers do not react to histamine;

hence, they are not involved in the typical histamine-caused inflammation (flare). There are many other conditions that stimulate these fibers, including certain skin conditions, chronic diseases, irritants, chemicals and damage to neurofibers in the brain.

Good news: Itch receptors are found only in the top two skin layers. "So what?" you might say. Well…you can feel a heartache, but never a heart itch or a kidney or liver itch. You get the point, don't you? How would you ever scratch your liver?

Noxious stimulation: There is one area where itch and pain interact. Strangely, pain—what researchers call "noxious stimulation"—can be used to reduce or stop histamine-caused itch by using the following: uncomfortable heat, electric shock, unpleasant chemicals, painful sensations, rubbing or scratching. The rub here is if any of the aforementioned stimuli are applied moderately, it doesn't work. But if it's really uncomfortable without being unbearable, researchers have recorded that the itch will disappear for at least thirty minutes. They cannot verify a longer period because, in a clinical setting, injected histamine quickly dissipates.[6] My experience with hot water or a hot hair dryer, on even very serious rashes, is complete itch cessation for at least seven hours—a full night's sleep. Of course, there are always exceptions. Not everyone has this positive of an experience with heat, Dr. Yosipovitch cautions.[2]

It is not yet known why noxious pain stops the itch, even though the Internet is ringing with chants of "Heat flushes the histamine right out of the skin." One person made it up, and it spread like an upended ice cream cone on a warm sidewalk. A couple of clinical studies came to the conclusion that the interaction is within the central nervous system, perhaps the spinal cord.[4, 7]

The Helpful Heat Technique For Itch Relief

COMPLETELY STOPS POISON OAK AND POISON IVY RASHES UP TO SEVEN HOURS FOR MOST PEOPLE

When researchers use the term "noxious heat," they are referring to heat applied at a temperature uncomfortable to the point of pain— "Yeoww"—but not hot enough to burn the skin. Yes, there have been studies on heat applied to itchy rashes.

According to a good many converts, heat works to completely stop the itching of a poison oak and poison ivy rash for up to seven hours. Researchers were a bit more subdued. "The present results show that heat pain...can attenuate (reduce) histamine-induced itch in healthy human subjects."[6]

I am familiar with many commercial and home remedies. Some reduce the itch for a couple of hours, which is acceptable in the daytime, but not when you crave a full night's sleep. In the 1970s I was extremely allergic to poison oak. Nights were torture until I discovered hot water. Recently I discovered the hair dryer technique online. I tried it and was impressed. With either technique, the temperature needs to be uncomfortably hot—almost painful. The itch will intensify for a couple of seconds before it disappears, although it's hard to tell at that point because the intensity of the heat overwhelms the itch. When you remove the heat, poof—no itch. Using insufficient heat will reduce the itch for a lessor amount of time.

Discussing treatments, a 1952 book on dermatology mentioned "very hot water" applications as "often the most effective measure to relieve itching."[12]

Internet posts discussing hot water and hair dryer heat are common these days. It seems many people are fans of this technique. Most believe the itch ceases because the heat forces the itch-causing chemical histamine from the skin. Not so according to researchers.[4, 7]

WARNING: It's possible to burn your skin with hot water or hot air. New skin in open blisters or lesions is especially fragile.

Supervise children carefully, using lower heat than for adult skin. I know a 10-year-old who burned his foot by using a hair dryer on his own. It didn't blister, but hurt for awhile.

Hair dryer: This works as well as hot water and is more convenient. You can easily reach any area on your body.

1. Highest setting. Simply run the heat back and forth over the rash and a little beyond. Move in closer until it is uncomfortably hot, but not hot enough to burn your skin. Usually it only takes a few seconds to feel results.

2. If you smell burning hair, you are too close.

3. Be extra careful over broken blisters. New skin burns easily.

4. The itch will intensify and then disappear. Continue a little longer, moving to outlying areas.

5. If you don't have a hair dryer, buy a little fold-up one to use when necessary. Extremely allergenic folks might want one for their travel kit.

6. Buy a cordless hair dryer for day trips and get up to eight minutes of heat touch-ups—that is, if you can afford the huge price. (See "Commercial Products.")

Hot water:

1. Don't think in terms of soaking in a tub of hot water or standing under a hot shower What I am discussing is water that will feel painful after more than a few seconds exposure— about 120°F. (Although some people say standing in a hot shower works for them, I don't consider it "working" unless you can sleep throughout the night).

2. Turn on hot water and move your rash in and out quickly, not allowing the skin to become burned.

3. For hard-to-reach areas, wet a cloth with hot water and imme-

diately lay it on the rash for a few seconds. This is a bit messy and the cloth cools off quickly. The process must be repeated multiple times.

4. In the shower, when the water is very hot, quickly move parts of your body in and out.

5. When camping, heat water over a fire and fill a metal water bottle to roll over the rash.

Electric-Battery heater:
I have a small hand-held heater. You can plug it in or use a nine-volt battery to heat up the quarter-size metal head. It's small, but if you move it around from place to place slowly, giving it enough time to transfer heat to your skin, it does an acceptable job of stopping the itch for a short time at least. It's handy for traveling in a plane or car, for example. No hot water? No electrical outlets? Screaming itch? Try this. (See "Commercial Products.")

Does cold work? Freezing cold stops the itch for awhile, then the skin warms up. Slight cooling and warm conditions have no effect.

Why is high heat is so effective? Researchers suspect the heat effect occurs somewhere up the nerve network—near the spine or higher—rather than the itch location. The full answer has not been found.[6]

Dr. Gil Yosipovitch is a dermatologist and well-known itch researcher. He cautioned me that heat does not work for everybody. Only about a third of his patients reported good results from hot showers. He works with many folks whose chronic itch sensation is manifested by the other of the two separate nerve pathways for itch, the pathway that does not react to histamine. This other pathway does not respond as well to heat when attempting to stop the itch. [2, 7]

THE HELPFUL HEAT TECHNIQUE FOR ITCH RELIEF does not assist healing or change the progression of the rash (at least not that I have experienced or heard of), but it will take care of the worst side effect of the allergic reaction and that's good enough for me.

CHOOSING REMEDIES

**When you burn or cut yourself, slam the door on your finger—
"Ow, ow, ow!"—it hurts like heck, but immediately the healing
process begins. Soon things are looking up. On the other hand,
an allergic poison oak and poison ivy dermatitis is very different. While you are applying anti-itch, healing and soothing remedies, the immune system is producing histamine and other
chemicals, injuring the skin even more. No wonder it seems
nothing is working. You can't keep up with the onslaught; your
remedies are not affecting the immune system itself. The rash
continues to worsen for days—often for over a week—before it
turns the corner and heads down the healing hill.**

Although I live in poison oak country, the variety of locally
available commercial remedies is meager. Ordering online is a
good option. I describe quite a few of the commercially available
products in "Commercial Products" at the back of the book, including contact information. Other possibilities are natural household products or dried herbs, either store-bought or, if you live in
the country, hand-picked. When all else fails, visit a physician or
alternative practitioner.

**Friends will recommend remedies that worked for them.
They may not work for you. Online discussions are hotbeds
of idiocy and downright wrong information interspersed with
good advice.**

WHAT YOU NEED TO KNOW *BEFORE* YOU HAVE TO DEAL WITH A RASH.

These subjects are covered more fully in other chapters. Reread
them if need be.

1. Identification: Learn to identify the allergenic plants in your
area.

2. Barrier: If you are extremely allergic, keep a barrier product
handy; it will trap the oil before it reaches your skin—hopefully.
One product (noted in "Commercial Products") was clinically stud-

ied to prove its effectiveness.

3. Plant removal: Learn how to suit up if you are on a mission.

4. Removing the oil from your skin after exposure

a. Dirt or clay: Learn the technique for using what is at hand in times of desperation.

b. Commercial oil remover: Choose the product you feel is best qualified to remove the allergenic oil. There are toxic and nontoxic choices. Keep one at home, in your backpack (light, not likely to spill, and easily used in the field), in your car and overnight kit.

5. Showering and laundering clothes: *Assume* you are contaminated and be very careful. Sloppiness can cause rashes in the darnedest places.

ASSESS YOUR LIFESTYLE

There are two very different types of individuals in regard to what they are willing to spread on their skin.

Type A are folks like me who eat organic foods, use natural skin products and buy earth-friendly goods. We always read labels.

Type B folks don't care one way or the other—whatever stops the itch. Having once been extremely allergic to poison oak, I remember rashes so terrible I would have poured jet fuel over my head if I was assured it would stop the torture. So there is no judgment here—just info.

DRY RUN

Let's do a dry run and see what you should do when you feel a rash coming on.

It's important to assemble products for each stage ahead of time, and plan for the worst.

1. First, wash your whole body *again* with a strong oil-removing product, assuming you missed spots the first time. It's crucial that you not touch contaminated clothing.

2. When your skin begins to redden and itch, it's hard to gauge the direction it will go. Will it be the King Kong of rashes, or wimp out after a few days? Of course, your rash history will give you a clue—but not always.

3 What you head for depends on whether you want to go non-toxic or potpourri.

4. If you are extremely sensitive, the rash seems to be coming on fast and strong and chemicals are okay, you could start with one of the products that claim to penetrate the skin, pull the oil out (even after the rash has begun), and promises to heal the rash quickly. This seems a bit much, but many people give testimony that it works for them.

5. For the label reader who shies away from petrochemicals and such, you can work with things like wet clay poultices, herbs with astringent qualities (usually containing tannic acid) and natural commercial products. Check out the mineral salts and soothing oatmeal soaks. Go to the folk remedy, diet and supplement chapters. There are some good herbal tinctures and other types of vehicles on the market. Consider visiting a homeopath, acupuncturist or naturopath.

6. When a medium rash has your nerves jangling by the end of the day, soothing baths, warm milk and cookies, plus an oral antihistamine to make you sleepy might be the ticket.

7. Remember, the rash will continually evolve. You will be busy changing techniques to meet each challenge.

Most important of all, bone up on THE HELPFUL HEAT TECHNIQUE FOR ITCH RELIEF discussed elsewhere in this book. It's your best hope for itch relief, especially at bedtime, freeing you up to concentrate on products that dry up blisters and soothe the skin.

PRODUCTS IN GENERAL
The efficiency of a product might be related to the vehicle for dispersing, the concentration and strength of the active ingre-

dients, or even the body location for application.

VEHICLE (Carrier of the product)

Solution: Liquids. Can be greasy, watery or contain alcohol. They might sting.

Gel: Some are alcohol-based and may cause dryness. Semisolid. Often sticky. Might sting.

Foam: Piles of tiny bubbles that soon pop and leave a thin, sticky solution.

Spray: Plunger dispensers. Efficient way to cover the area without touching the skin with your hands, but a bit wasteful.

Ointment: Greasy (like Vaseline) or creamy. Emulsions of water droplets suspended in oil. Moisturizing. Messy. Most effective formula for penetrating the skin.

Cream: Semisolid. Oil-based or water-based emulsions. Vanish when rubbed in. Less greasy than ointments. Can sting. More likely to cause an allergy from preservatives and fragrances.

Lotion: Thicker than solutions but will still pour. Some are suspensions of powder in water. As water evaporates, cooling creates itch relief. Fine powder is deposited on the skin. Calamine lotion is a well-known example.

Emollients: Contain substances such as lipids that seal in moisture and allow skin to repair.

MODE OF ACTION OF THE PRODUCT

As your rash develops, you will need to change the remedy to match the condition of your skin.

Before contamination

Blocking: Prevents allergenic oil from touching skin.

After contamination

Removal: Removes allergenic oil from the skin.

Deep removal: Some product labels state that they pull the allergenic oil back from underlying skin layers in hours to a day after contamination.

During the rash

Astringent: Causes contraction of body tissues and blood vessels to close off secretions. Plants with astringent qualities: Alum, amaranth, bayberry, buckthorn, cinquefoil, coffee, pearly everlasting, golden rod, grindelia, henna, Labrador tea, madrone, manzanita, myrrh, oak, persimmon (unripe), plantain, ragweed, sanicle, septfoil, sumac berries, tansy, tea, water lily root, wild geranium root, wild indigo, witch hazel, jewelweed,

Powder: Sops up liquid from drippy blisters.

Antiseptic: Kills bacteria.

Itch-relieving. Stops the itch. May contain chemicals and petrochemicals, or natural products and herbs, or even a mixture of all of the above. Unfortunately, most products are not totally successful for everybody (if they help at all). The worse the rash, the less success you will have. Luckily you can resort to THE HELPFUL HEAT TECHNIQUE FOR ITCH RELIEF.

Soothing: Soothes inflamed skin and promotes healing.

Cool or cold: Cool (menthol, phenol) and cold (freezer packs) can override the itch for a short while.

Counterirritant: Has an irritating quality that can cover the itch. Short lasting.

Moisturizing: Helps prevent drying and painful cracking of skin while blisters heal.

Stops the immune system reaction: Corticosteroids stop the progression of a rash. Only prescription products are considered strong enough to be effective. If you start, you need to continue until the rash is healed. If you stop, the immune system will ramp up again. Doses are by injection, pills or cream.

Antihistamine: Helps stop the production of histamine, but not effective with poison oak and poison ivy rash because other itch causing chemicals are also released into the skin. The older types that cause drowsiness are sometimes used as a sleep aid during the rash.

Healing: Aids damaged skin.

Product labels claim amazing results. After testing quite a few on my friends, my family and myself, and after visiting Internet poison oak and poison ivy discussion sites, it is clear that very few (if any) products can quell the itch completely for a long period of time, although some products are quite a bit more popular than others.

Be forewarned when listening to other folks. It's common for a product that supposedly worked exceptionally well for one person to do nothing for another. If the allergic reaction is on the downswing anyway, any remedy will get high points for a job it didn't do.

SOME COMMON INGREDIENTS IN MANY COMMERCIAL PRODUCTS FOR ITCH RELIEF

Alcohol: Besides killing bacteria, alcohol has astringent properties that help dry blisters. As alcohol evaporates, it produces a cooling effect.

Antihistamine in a cream: Can cause a skin rash. Not considered effective anyway.

Benzocaine: Anesthetic. Can cause a skin rash.

Calamine: Zinc oxide and iron dioxide mixed together as a powder. This is the active ingredient in calamine lotion. It is used to sop up weeping blisters. I found it messy.

Camphor: A white, crystalline substance with an aromatic smell, occurring in certain essential oils and the camphor tree. It is also made synthetically. Camphor is readily absorbed through the skin and produces a feeling of cooling similar to that of menthol. It also acts like a slight local anesthetic by soothing itch and is antimicrobial. Because camphor is poisonous and absorbs into the skin, it must be diluted 11% in skin care products. It is used for acne and other skin conditions. Don't use it on children.

Cortisone cream 1%: This over-the-counter product is considered too weak a concentration to be effective on anything beyond a minor itch, but one woman told me it worked great on her medium rash. You would need to use it for the term of the rash to prevent a rebound effect.

Menthol: Has anesthetic and counterirritant qualities along with a cooling sensation. It is extracted from peppermint plants, but synthetic menthol is usually used in most products and seems to have low toxicity.

Oats: Soothing. In the bath or added to bar soap.

Phenol: Gives a cooling sensation like menthol. Another name is carbolic acid and it is corrosive to skin. Strangely, it is an ingredient in certain anti-itch creams. Obviously it is highly diluted.

Tannin: Often added to a product by including an herb that is high in tannin.

Zinc acetate: Besides being a dietary supplement, zinc acetate is often added to anti-itch ointments. It is an astringent.

MEDICAL PRESCRIPTIONS

Corticosteroids

Cortisone, hydrocortisone and prednisone are in the corticosteroid class of drugs, often used as anti-inflammatories and suppressors of the immune system. They are dispensed as injections, pills or creams.

Corticosteroids are often the ticket for the patient with a really bad rash. **"Do something—I can't stand it anymore."** Prednisone is popular.

There are problems, though. These meds work by damping down your immune system. The symptoms you have been experiencing are caused by the immune system ramping up, so if it's repressed by a corticosteroid, the symptoms disappear. But the immune system now might be too sluggish to respond to a real enemy, a virus, for example. The second problem is if the dosage is too weak, or the patient doesn't take as directed, there might be a rebound effect and the rash will flare up as badly as before. You will need to start the meds over from day one. A typical prescription gives a progression of weaker doses so the adrenals can get back to speed by the end of the dosage, for example, 60 mg x two to three days, then 40 mg x three days, 20 mg x three days, 10 mg x three days.

Before corticosteroids existed, a horrible case of poison oak or poison ivy rash might result in death from kidney damage, or an inflamed throat or lungs. Now, they would probably hook you up to a prednisone IV and let'er drip.

Corticosteroid creams are prescribed as a lower potency alternative to pills or injection, and can be up to 600 times stronger than hydrocortisone creams sold over-the-counter.

Each physician has his or her favorite prescription for poison oak or poison ivy rashes. One doctor I spoke to said there are always new pharmaceuticals on the market. He prescribes an older generic product introduced in the 50s, triamcinolone acetate. It's available in various strengths, and can be purchased as a cheap generic prescription.

There are many possible side effects from these creams, increasing as the potency of the prescription increases. One side effect mimics the rash you are attempting to heal, causing a rash over the rash.

There are many over-the-counter hydrocortisone creams available, but these are considered too weak to have any affect.

Antihistamines

Shouldn't antihistamines be the perfect medication to stop a rash? After all, their job is to stop the production of histamine, which causes the itching. Apparently they don't work well with poison oak and poison ivy rashes. The book *Fisher's Contact Dermatitis* says "...although they inhibit mast cell and basophile function, they do not appreciably alter contact hypersensitivity."[7] There are more itch-causing chemicals released than just histamine. It seems that the type of antihistamines that make you drowsy are prescribed for bedtime to help the sufferer sleep instead of for an antihistamine effect.

Topical antihistamines (creams) also have a poor reputation. They should be avoided because of the potential for allergy sensitization.[8]

FOLK REMEDIES

Folk remedies have one thing in common with commercial remedies. They work amazingly well for some folks and not at all for others. People write the darndest things on Internet discussion sites, for instance the claim that white shoe polish did an overnight job of curing the rash, while giving a darn good shine to new skin. (I embellished the claim a bit).

It's amazing how many medicinal plants grow right under our noses. I have six of the listed plants growing wild on my five acres in southern Oregon and four in my garden.

Many of the following herbs have astringent qualities, usually from tannin. When the blisters break, the liquid is very messy. Astringents help to close off the secretions.

BOTANICALS

Alder: The bark helps dry the rash. Boil in water and apply when cool.

Aloe vera: Very popular, especially soothing on the face. It's also a good carrier of other herbs and medication into the skin. Buy the gel or grow your own plant. Cut the skin of the leaf to access the gel. Many nurseries sell this plant.

Alumroot: The root is very astringent and styptic. Make a tincture or boil into a strong tea.

Amaranth (pigweed): The leaves of this prolific weed are astringent and help reduce tissue swelling. Make a tea or apply the wet leaves.

Bay leaves: Boil the leaves and apply as a poultice, or soak a cloth in the tea and apply to the rash.

Beech: A Native American remedy. Boil the bark in water and apply the liquid.

Catnip: Drink the tea for relaxing and sleeping. Rub crushed leaves on the rash.

Chickweed: This weed grows in many yards. It is known to be soothing to itchy skin.

Chlorophyll: The chlorophyll in wheat grass is healing and antiseptic. Some natural food stores sell fresh wheat grass juice.

Dock: Yellow dock, curly leaf dock, sour dock, and broad-leafed dock. The root of this common weed is very medicinal. A recipe from the eighteen hundreds says to bruise fresh leaves, simmer in sweet cream, butter or lard, and eat---I mean apply to the rash.

Echinacea: This is a powerful anti-inflammatory herb. Among other things, it is used for skin conditions. Take two capsules of the powdered root every two hours or make a tea and drink, applying the liquid also to the rash. The root has been used in homeopathic preparations for poison oak and poison ivy rashes.

Flax oil: Effective for the swelling caused by inflammation. Apply the oil to the rash.

Gatrlic: Boil a cup of water and add four chopped cloves of garlic. Let cool and apply to the rash. Repeat often. Drink garlic tea. Ugh. Don't make a date with that special person for a while.

Goldenseal: This is considered a very healing herb. The dried powder is said to have antibiotic and astringent (not from tannin) qualities and will dry up the moisture of an open sore. I noticed years ago that scrapes covered with goldenseal powder dried up quickly. Moisten the powder and apply to open blisters, or apply a tincture.

Grindelia (gumweed): This herb is often mentioned as being effective in stopping the itch. California Native Americans used it. The astringent property comes from tannin. The leaves and flowers are used. The plant is covered with a sticky resin. Flowers are yellow, and it grows in dry areas in the western U.S. Cut off the top third of the plant, put in boiling water and simmer for thirty minutes, or make a tincture.

Jewelweed: Touch-me-not, snapweed. This plant grows in the eastern part of the U.S. and is the most popular herbal remedy in the east. It grows up to four feet. The flowers are yellowish orange and the juice from the stems and leaves is light orange. In the nineteen sixties, well known herbalist Euell Gibbons praised this herb. As a preventive for anyone returning from a hike, he boiled the plant in water, and then added the orange liquid to the bath, or dabbed it directly on rashes. Juice from the crushed leaves or stems can be smoothed on the skin as a preventive when you brush against a plant. You can boil up a pot of jewelweed and make ice cubes to rub over the rash. Another recipe is to simmer (without boiling) in enough oil to cover, for thirty minutes and strain. Keep refrigerated. A tincture of jewelweed though, will keep indefinitely. The distinctive orange-colored juice, called lawsone, contains tannin. Lawsone is also in henna, the powdered root that gives brown hair red highlights and makes grey hair orange.

An herbalist told me that in his experience, jewelweed usually works well up to the third or forth poison ivy rash, and then with succeeding rashes, seems to lose its oomph.

I fear you now need to hear another story. Poison ivy researcher David Senchina wrote in 2005 that Jewelweed "has been discredited by a number of studies as a remedy for poison ivy rash.[9] Cock your ear and you can hear jewelweed fans loudly booing. I have no experience with the plants (I live in the Northwest), but if they contain lots of tannin—they should at least have *some* astringent qualities. Besides, there must be *some* reason why jewelweed has such a sterling reputation. It even conveniently lives in the same neighborhoods as poison ivy.

Madrone: This tree has a reddish bark that continually peels off. Red berries dot the tree in the fall. Boil madrone bark for a while and apply the tea to the rash.

Manzanita: This shrub grows in dry areas. It's related to madrone. Make a strong tea with bark or leaves.

Mugwort: This herb is often mentioned. Make a strong tea or tincture and apply to the skin.

Mullein: Anti inflammatory. Flowers are preferred, but juice from the leaves may be applied to the skin or used in tinctures or creams.

Myrrh: Anti inflammatory, anesthetic, pain killing and anti-bacterial.

Nervines: The horrible itching of a bad case of poison oak or ivy can make anybody extremely irritable. Even something as simple as mint or chamomile tea is soothing, but other herbs are somewhat more effective. This is a strong recipe: Equal parts of black cohash root, cayenne, hops, lady's slipper root, lobelia, skullcap, valerian, wood betony, mistletoe. Put in capsules or make a tincture.

Oak: The leaves, acorns and bark of the oak tree contain lots of tannic acid. With a serious rash, the seeping blisters are a big problem. Herbs containing tannic acid are added to some of the commercial poison oak and poison ivy products because of its astringent quality. It helps to dry the oozing blisters and reduce inflammation and swelling. Make a strong tea of oak bark or leaves and apply to the skin. An old folk recipe was to chop a half a milk pail full of oak bark (Hack at limbs, not trunk), Boil for an hour and soak in the bathtub as long as possible. This was once a popular rememby.

Oatmeal: Oatmeal is very soothing to the skin. Grind up oats, put them in a sock, and put in the tub to sooth a head to toe rash. There is also a commercial product composed of ground oats.

Peppermint: Contains menthol which creates a cooling affect, but the effect doesn't last very long. Commercial remedies usually contain synthetic menthol.

Persimmon: An unripe persimmon is so astringent it makes your mouth pucker. Spread the pulp over the rash. Cover with a cloth or plastic.

Plantain: There are over 200 species of this prolific plant. I see this herb mentioned often as being helpful for poison oak and poison ivy rashes. The leaves radiate from the base and are considered very healing to the skin. Mash the fresh leaves, apply and cover to keep moist. Reapply before it dries.

Prickly ash: Native Americans used the inner bark of this shrub boiled in water to treat itches. It grows in sandy dry areas in the southern states.

Ragweed: This plant is a problem to hay fever sufferers, but has also been used to cure poison oak and poison ivy rashes because of its astringent and antiseptic qualities. Make a poultice of the crushed leaves.

Tansy: This herb grows to three feet. It has featherlike leaves and flat button-like gold flowers. The crushed plant has an aromatic smell and a bitter taste. It contains tannic acid, creating its astringent effect. All parts of the plant can be used. Bathe the skin with the strong tea.

Black tea: Use the boiled leaves of black tea as a poultice to access the astringent tannic acid.

Vinegar: When I was very sensitive to poison oak, apple cider vinegar worked as well for me as rubbing alcohol, except that I smelled like a tossed green salad. I suppose the garlic remedy should go along with this for a mouth-watering effect. White distilled vinegar might work as well without the smell.

Witch hazel: The fluid extract of witch hazel is prized as an astringent with anti-inflammatory and wound healing qualities. I read that the tannins are often lost in the distillation. Instead of going to the pharmacy, look for the dried herb or tincture in herb or natural food stores. Make your own tincture if necessary

Yerba Santa: This herb has been mentioned often as a cure for poison oak. The leaves are covered with resin. Boil a large amount of leaves to make a concentrated liquid and apply to the rash

NON-BOTANICALS

Alcohol: Rubbing alcohol is the cheapest, but the drinkable kind will work. When I was very sensitive to poison oak, I carried a small bottle of rubbing alcohol with me to pat on itchy spots. It evaporates quickly, cooling the skin. Alcohol is drying to skin besides being antiseptic. Making a tincture with the herbs of your choice would add to its effectiveness.

Baking soda: This remedy is messy if you mix with water and make a mud. It falls off in big clumps. But, try a thin wash of baking soda over your rash, or ½ cup added to your bath water to sooth the skin.

Bleach: Diluted sodium hypochlorite is the form of chlorine in liquid household bleach. It is also used in pools. Some people swear that soaking in a swimming pool will cure your rash within a few days. Fine. Safe enough. But others tout something scary—rub straight bleach on your rash. A fellow on an Internet discussion site said it burns really bad—but he suggested it anyway. Someone else wrote that his mother had scars for life from doing this.

A fellow wrote on an Internet discussion site that he sits for 15 to 20 minutes in a cool bath after pouring a quart of bleach in it. He said to get ready to "SCREAM!...it's going to hit you like battery acid." You are instructed to do it again in a few hours. This is not an isolated nut. I saw a couple more accounts like the above, with hollering and everything. I also met a nice man who insisted that "everybody does it" in his hometown. It's a well-known folk remedy. Even the kids are dunked in, left with a fan to blow the fumes away, dabbed off gently without rinsing and thrown back in the next day if needed. He understatement was, "Sure it hurt." He hasn't heard of any medical problems from the technique.

The above folk remedy apparently works to quickly put a halt to the pesky itch, but what a gamble. Chlorine bleach is caustic. It can cause significant irritation and burns. The bleach will continue burning until it is removed by flushing with water. In cases of fume inhalation, there may be shallow breathing, paleness or fainting.

Clay: I talked about clay earlier. Carry it with you and spread it on your skin for an absorbent barrier. Rub the clay briskly over your skin if you bump into a poison oak or poison ivy plant. Pat dry clay over seeping blisters, and/or use as a damp poultice over a rash.

Cold: Run ice cubes over the rash, or buy a large ice pack. Cold has been clinically proven to stop the itch, but not for long.

Epsom salts: (magnesium sulfate). I would never be without Epsom salts. I have successfully used these salts for deep infections on horses and goats for the "drawing" healing quality. For a serious head to toe rash, I would suggest using THE HELPFUL HEAT TECHNIQUE FOR ITCH RELIEF and then soaking a bath with a few cups of Epsom salts to help dry up the rash.

Hydrogen peroxide: I have seen this stuff dry up bedsores on invalids within a couple of days. It's powerful. On open blisters it is worth a try. If you have never used it before, it is entertaining to watch it bubble and fizz.

Ocean: Jump in the ocean. Confirmed ocean jumpers insist it must be the real thing but a pile of sea salt in tub water might do the trick. Sea salt helps dry up weepy blisters, although I think Epsom salts are stronger.

Urine, horse: I have read about this remedy numerous times. I have no clue why cow, goat or pig urine wouldn't work. Wear a pair of tall galoshes when collecting.

Urine, your own: (variation—urine with spit) Now you see how desperate some people become. The whole idea is poppycock—and smelly. Phoo!

SUGGESTIONS FROM FOLKS WHO WANT TO HAVE THEIR REMEDY AND EAT IT TOO

Cucumber: Rub soothing cucumber over the rash, then make a salad. No, with the leftover cucumber.

Celery: Dab the juice on your rash. Add celery chunks to the cucumber salad.

Vinegar: Put vinegar on your skin. Now put vinegar on your cucumber and celery salad (balsamic vinegar is a good choice).

Salt: Sprinkle a little salt on your salad—now on your open blisters. Oh, did that sting? How about a little spritz of lemon juice.

Canned pineapple: Sorry, nothing funny about this. Just plop one of those doughnut shaped slices on and tie with a string.

Prepared mustard: "Pardon me, would you have any Grey Poupon?"

Meat tenderizer: "After you finish with the steaks, would you sprinkle some on my arm?"

Oatmeal: Have some for breakfast, and smear the rest on your rash.

Miracle Whip: "Don't give me the good stuff, it has to be Miracle Whip."

Buttermilk: Drink some (no thanks, yuck). Dab on rash.

Honey: Honey in your hair. That's what will happen if you try smearing honey anywhere. It always ends up in your hair. Trust me, I was a beekeeper.

Mixture of okra and bear grease: First shoot a bear...

WEIRD REMEDIES

Gunpowder

Hair spray

Brake cleaner

White shoe polish

Toothpaste

Cigar ashes and saliva: First smoke the cigar and then spit a lot.

MAKING HERBAL TINCTURES

It's fun to make tinctures, especially if you are familiar with herbs growing in your area. Herb or natural foods stores sell dried herbs. I like to dry my wild-picked herbs so the water in the leaves won't dilute the alcohol. Use a sunny window or an electric food dehydrator.

Tinctures

You can use vinegar, but alcohol is considered best for tinctures. Vodka works well, but since you will not be ingesting the formula, rubbing alcohol is acceptable. By itself, alcohol often is used to stop the itch and help dry oozing blisters. With herbs, the effect will be enhanced.

Herbalist Kami McBride has a few poison oak and poison ivy tincture remedies on her Web site. Each recipe uses equal amounts of herbs and you only need a small amount, enough to reach the top of the liquid. Less than a quarter cup of liquid should be plenty. Shake the jar each day for two weeks. Strain.

- Poison Oak Ease: Yerba santa, oak leaf, mugwort.
- Oak Away: Witch hazel, myrrh, yerba santa.
- Poison Oak Wash: Manzanita, echinacea root, mugwort.[10]

DIET AND SUPPLEMENTS

Histamine is an immune system chemical that causes skin inflammation along with itching during allergic dermatitis. Certain foods contain histamine or cause the body to release histamine when ingested. It makes sense to cut down on diet-caused histamine release when you are dealing with an immune condition that is also releasing histamine.

Histamine-rich foods

Foods to omit while the rash is active

Alcoholic beverages, anchovies, avocados, cheeses (especially aged or fermented), cider, dried fruits, eggplant, pickles, smoked meats, mushrooms, processed meats (sausage, hot dogs, etc.), sardines, smoked fish, sour cream, yogurt, soured breads, spinach, tomatoes, vinegar.

Histamine-releasing foods

Alcohol, bananas, chocolate, eggs, fish, milk, papayas, pineapple, shellfish, strawberries, tomatoes.

Antihistamine action by herbs and foods

Some foods and herbs show natural antihistamine action in lab studies, although there are few clinical trials using humans.

Foods to add while the rash is active

Vitamin C: Considered to have antihistamine properties. Take a lot. It's safe.

Butterbur: Available as a pill in herb or natural food stores.

Mangosteen: A fruit extract usually sold as a juice. Capsules also are available. This fruit has been shown to possibly inhibit release of histamine.

Nettles: Sold in pill form.

Noni fruit juice: A tropical fruit.

Quercetin: This is a bioflavonoid. It helps block the release of histamine. Take 500 mg twice daily.

Bromelain: Will enhance the absorption of quercetin. Take 100 mg twice daily.

Eliminating diet

An alternative medicine practitioner might suggest a cooling elimination diet of dark green vegetables, fruits, raw nuts, fish, and soups. It will act as an anti-inflammatory in the system.

Foods to omit: Red meat, saturated fats, soft drinks, coffee, white flour, sugar, spicy foods, curry.

ACUPUNCTURE

Acupuncturists practice Traditional Chinese Medicine, an ancient practice based on the natural rhythms of life. Treatment will probably include Chinese herbs (sometimes western herbs), acupuncture and lifestyle consultation.[11]

Acupuncturists with whom I spoke in Oregon do treat poison oak rashes. They use acupuncture, especially in the early stages of the rash, and find Chinese herbs also to be effective for this condition. Packaged formulas are available, but a special formula might be mixed for you. And, because a poison oak rash is considered a heat condition, you probably will be encouraged to abstain from spicy and sour foods.

If you prefer a natural practitioner, an acupuncturist is not only a good choice, but this method of treatment also is covered under many medical insurance policies.

HOMEOPATHY

Homeopathy treats disease by stimulating the immune system with highly diluted substances that, in large amounts, produce symptoms similar to those being treated. Since the dilutions are considered pharmacologically free of plant molecules, they are considered safe.

If you develop a serious case of poison oak or poison ivy, visit a homeopathic practitioner for a thorough evaluation and an individualized formula. I know a few people who regularly visit homeopaths and are very happy with the results.

Although not recommended by most practitioners, over-the-counter homeopathic remedies are available at natural foods stores and many pharmacies. The homeopathic remedy prepared from poison ivy leaves is called *Rhus tox*. This is short for *Rhus toxicodendron*, an older botanical name for poison ivy (now called *Toxicodendron radicans*).

There are at least three types of products containing *Rhus tox*. All are taken orally.

1. One product claims to relieve the itching, burning and crusting of a poison oak and poison ivy rash, and mixes *Rhus tox* with two other remedies that are specific for these symptoms. See the commercial products section at the back of the book.

2. Another company sells a liquid dilution of *Rhus tox*, with the dosage specifically designed for developing a resistance to the plant's allergenic oil. It is often taken in early spring and throughout the summer, but the dose can be continued every day or so to extend the resistance. The package states it also can be taken to relieve itching from an existing rash. See "Resources."

3. Homeopathic *Rhus tox* is considered a remedy for the pain of arthritis and tendonitis. It is sold in pill and liquid form.

STATE OF MIND

In the 1970s, I joked about the psychic dentist who rolled into town claiming he could turn your fillings to gold, and smirked about the guru who would teach you how to eat air for sustenance. But what got my dander up were those folks who were convinced that anyone could prevent those darned poison oak rashes by becoming psychically one with the plant. Hogwash!

State of mind, as a part of one's whole organism, does play an important part in the maintenance of equilibrium. It's becoming increasingly clear that mental states can influence the immune system. But if a person has no predisposition for developing an allergy, he or she can be in terrible shape mentally and not be affected by a substance that would knock another person around the block.

I once had a horse. I respected her strength and huge size. She could squash me against a fence or mash my foot flat, but I was not afraid of her. I knew her ways—I was *mindful*. It's called "horse sense."

I developed my poison oak Automatic Sensor by learning poison oak's ways and being mindful. I took my lumps and slowly became somewhat tolerant. I was never nervous about entering poison oak territory. I even potted a plant for my windowsill. I smiled when my son-in-law, after an uncomfortable rash, stated, "I'm not going to live my life in fear of those plants," and marched out the door to continue weed whacking in the poison oak patch. There is no woo-woo stuff here, just a mindful attitude and a positive state of mind.

References

1. Paus, Ralf, et al. 2006. "Frontiers in Pruritus Research: Scratching the Brain for More Effective Itch Therapy." *J Clin Invest* 116(5):1174-118.

2. Ikoma, Akihiko, Martin Steinhoff, Sonja Stander, Gill Yosipovitch, and Martin Schmelz. 2006. "The Neurobiology of Itch." *Nature Reviews*, vol. 7.

3. Ward, Louise. 1996. "A Comparison of the Effects of Noxious and Innocuous Counter Stimuli on Experimentally Induced Itch and Pain." *Pain* 64:129-138.

4. Johanek, Lisa M., Richard A. Meyer, Tim Hartke, Joseph G. Hobelmann, David N. Maine, Robert H. LaMotte, and Matthias Ringkamp. 2007. "Psychophysical and Physiological Evidence of Parallel Afferent Pathways Mediating the Sensation of Itch." *Journal of Neuroscience* July 11.

5. Yosipovitch, G., M.I. Duque, K. Fast, A.G. Dawn, and R.C. Coghill. 2007. "Scratching

and Noxious Heat Stimuli Inhibit Itch in Humans: A Psychophysical Study." *British Journal of Dermatology* 156:629-634.

6. Shim, Won-Sik, and Uhtaek Oh. 2008. "Histamine-Induced Itch and Its Relationship with Pain." *Molecular Pain* 4:29.

7. Yosipovitch, Gil. 2010. Itch researcher, Forest Univ. School of Medicine. Phone interview. Salem, NC.

8. Resnick, Steven D. 1986. "Poison-Ivy and Poison-Oak Dermatitis." *Clinics in Dermatology* 4(2): April-June. 208-212.

9. Senchina, David S. 2005. "A Critical Review of Herbal Remedies for Poison Ivy Dermatitis." *HerbalGram* 66:35-48.

10. McBride, Kami. 2010. "Poison Oak and Poison Ivy." www.livingawareness.com.

11. Tierra, Michael, and Leslie Tierra. 1998. *Chinese Traditional Herbal Medicine*. Lotus Press, WI.

Sam's "perfect state of mind"
begins to falter.

Chapter 12

THE MANY USES FOR THE PLANTS

PAST USES BY NATIVE AMERICANS

Although Native Americans considered poison ivy, poison oak and poison sumac rather dangerous, they found it helpful in various aspects of their lives. The following examples are from the book *Native American Ethnobotany*.[1] I chose these because the author used material published by researchers who themselves worked with Native American tribes.

MEDICINE

- Buds eaten in the spring to obtain immunity from the plant poisons. Tolowa people.
- Strong tea for sores inside eyelids, and to improve vision. Diegueño people.
- Leaf eaten as a contraceptive. Karok people. (Before you try it, this doesn't mean it works.)
- Plant juice applied to warts. I know this works because I cured my own wart this way. It disappeared slowly over a couple of months. Mendocino people.
- Fresh leaf poultice for rattlesnake bite. Wailaki people.
- Strong tea to induce vomiting. Cherokee people.
- Poultice of fresh or roasted crushed roots, and salve containing

root placed on skin to heal injury, running sores, inflammation, and to cause a swelling to open (a boil, for example). Delaware, Oklahoma, Meskwaki, Iroquois peoples.

- Sedative for children. Iroquois people.
- Wash for skin infections. Cherokee people.
- Taken in some form for fever. Cherokee people.
- Taken in some form for asthma. Cherokee people.
- Taken in some form for bladder problems. Cherokee people.
- Taken in some form for venereal disease. People not noted.
- Strong tea of leaves as a rejuvenating tonic. Houma people.
- Leaves rubbed on skin affected by a poison ivy reaction. Algonquin people. (I'm just repeating what the researcher said.)
- Plant used for running or nonhealing sores. Kiowa people.

DYE, DECORATION
- Charcoal or soot used to color objects black.
- Ashes used to darken skin of mixed blood children. Pomo people.
- Ashes made into a paste for tattooing. Pomo people.
- Black sap for tattoos. Mendocino people.
- Juice used to dye leaves of blackroot sedge for baskets. Pomo people.
- Ashes of the wood made into a paste for tattooing. Pomo and Kashaya peoples.

COOKING
- Leaves used to wrap acorn meal for baking. Mendocino people.
- Twigs used to spit fish while smoking. Karok people.
- Branches and twigs used to cook and smoke salmon. Karok people.

CONTAINERS

- Stems used in basketry. Costanoan and Mendocino peoples.
- Leaves used to cover soap plant while cooking in the earth oven. Karok people.
- Leaves used to wrap bread. Costanoan people.

ECOLOGICAL BENEFITS

These beautiful, fantastic plants are here to stay. They certainly rule the roost on my five acres.

If a group formed proposing to eradicate huge swaths of poison oak and poison ivy, scientists would suddenly appear with cautions like this from researcher David Senchina: "Imprudent destruction of *Toxicodendron* populations could result in loss of food and/or shelter for birds, fungi, arthropods, and mammals, with consequent indirect effects on other taxa associated with these organisms."[2]

Poison oak and poison ivy are home, sweet home and sustenance for many animals, especially deer. In a symbiotic relationship, bees gather nectar as they rush from blossom to blossom transporting pollen. Nineteen fungus species grow among poison oak and poison ivy plants; some are beneficial to the plants, some not. Insects munch the leaves, leaving openings for the allergenic resin to reach the surface. Birds appreciate the fruits of poison oak and poison ivy, obligingly scattering the seeds with their droppings. Small mammals find shelter in the foliage.[2]

When a large area of land is cleared, either by humans or a huge slide, for example, poison oak and poison ivy are one of the first plants to take hold and stabilize the soil. In 1994, Janet Howard, writing for the Department of Agriculture, stated, "Poison oak has been recommended for use in restoration projects...Having worked on field crews in the Sierra Nevada foothills, however, this author recommends, using native shrubs other than poison oak for restoration."[3]

Maybe there were uprisings among crews, because I searched for a poison oak propagating nursery to no avail. Another problem could have been the difficulty propagating poison oak and poison ivy. First the seed needs to be scratched or dropped into a hot bath and left to soak for a few days. Even with coddling, only three out of a hundred seeds actually sprout. Then they must survive to adulthood. Digging up rhizomes is an option, but these tend to have big problems with a fungus, which kills off most of the plants in the greenhouse. Usually, only about six out of a hundred rhizomes survive.[4] All of this hassle and disappointment over a plant that is almost impossible to eradicate once it is established.

When you begin to lose heart during a raging rash, remember the millions of *Toxicodendrons* clambering around the countryside of America pumping out life-giving oxygen. Think about the unstable hillsides propped up by multitudes of poison oak and poison ivy roots.

PRESENT MEDICAL USES

Oriental Medicine

While a goodly number of Americans consider urushiol (the allergenic oil of poison oak and poison ivy) to be at the same level as Satan, Koreans eat it from a related tree, the Japanese lacquer tree, as a spring tonic or for gastrointestinal problems, often in a savory chicken stew. Yes, some folks *do* break out in rashes and visit medical clinics, but leave undaunted. They are not about to give up their spring tonic.[5]

Lest you doubt my research, I found a list on the Internet of local restaurants participating in a 2009 archeological festival in Korea. One restaurant listed "Native chicken steamed with *Lacquer Poison*" as an example of a main dish.

Bits of leaves and twigs of the allergenic tree can be thrown in with the chicken, but many cooks apparently want simplicity. Because there is always an entrepreneur on the sidelines ready to supply any demand—voila! *Lacquer Poison Resin*. This was available at the fourth annual 2006 Korean Consumer Products Expo, packaged up and ready to "poison" the stew. Yummy.

Homeopathic poison ivy

Rhus tox, the highly diluted homeopathic formula made from poison ivy leaves, is a remedy for the pain of arthritis, sciatica, joints, tendonitis, and the itch of chicken pox. *Rhus tox* also is a remedy for its own symptoms: the itch of poison oak and poison ivy. Besides being an aid in soothing an itching rash, clinical studies have shown that another product (with a stronger-than-normal dilution of poison ivy) is effective in creating seasonal tolerance to poison oak and poison ivy when taken in early spring through the summer. (See "Commercial Products.)"

Poison oak flower essence

I have a small bottle of poison oak flower essence. The tiny flowers were infused in water, and a tad of brandy was added as a preservative. The dose is two drops in water taken four times daily for a month. Flower essences do not cure, but are designed to aid the inward-reflecting individual by stimulating awareness of emotion and physical body. Poison oak flower essence is specified for those with a fear of intimate contact—those protective of personal boundaries.

Only tiny traces of the poison oak flower are detectable in the product; hence, it is considered nontoxic. I suspect the allergic oil urushiol is minutely present in the remedy since it is present in the flowers.

Flower essences are dispensed most often by "natural practitioners" who work with the whole person, not just the symptoms.

THE FUTURE

Medical possibilities

In a previous chapter, I documented claims by physicians (in the late 1700s to the early 1900s) of the amazing healing powers of urushiol, and we all had a good laugh. Actually, there is a grain of truth.

Koreans have been particularly active in studying the Japanese lacquer tree. The urushiol of the tree has almost the same chemistry as the urushiols of poison oak and poison ivy. In 2001 Korean researchers concluded that urushiol might have potential as an effective antitumor agent in the treatment of ovarian cancer. It seems that urushiol triggers the death of the cancer cells.[6] In 2010 researchers deemed urushiol effective in eradication or reduction of *H. pylori*, the bacteria that causes gastritis and ulcers. They admitted, though, that the itchy rashes could be a problem.[7]

Dr. Alain Martin has an interesting patented and tested product ready for market: The allergenic oil urushiol, combined with a cream, will be applied to skin cancers in conjunction with a vaccine or other treatment to assist in eliciting an effective immune response. (Urushiol, isolated from poison ivy leaves, stimulates the immune system.) Clinical studies with humans showed that Dr Martin's formulation reduced basal cell carcinoma lesion size and, in combination with other therapies, "a complete elimination of the lesions occurred."[8]

I'd love to see the tides turn and people speaking of poison oak and poison ivy with reverence. "Did you hear? It cures cancer."

Climate change

In 2006, there was a flurry of excitement about a new study. It seems that along with climate change, carbon dioxide levels will rise. Because of this, by the middle of this century American Toxicodendrons (poison oak, poison ivy, poison sumac) not only will increase in growth by 149 percent, but the allergenic oil also will become even more powerful.

The plants will rule the countryside.[9]

References

1. Moerman, Daniel E. 1998. *Native American Ethnobotany*. Timber Press, Inc., Portland, OR.

2. Senchina, David S. 2008. "Fungal and Animal Associates of Toxicodendron spp. (Anacardiaceae) in North America." *Perspectives in Plant Ecology, Evolution and Systematics* 10:197-216.

3. Howard, Janet L. 1994. *Index of Species Information. Species: Diversilobum*. US Dept. of Agriculture Pamphlet.

4. Crosby, Donald G. 2004. *The Poisoned Weed*. Oxford University Press, NY.

5. Park, S.D., S.W. Lee, J.H. Chun, and S.H. Cha. 2000. "Clinical Features of Thirty One Patients with Systemic Contact Dermatitis due to the Ingestion of Rhus (Lacquer)." *British Journal of Dermatology* 142:937-942.

6. Choi, Ju-Youn, Chang-Soo Park, Jongoh Choi, Hyangshuk Rhim, and Jae Chun Heung. 2001. "Cytotoxic Effects of Urushiol on Human Ovarian Cancer Cells." *Journal of Microbiology and Biotechnology* 11:399-405.

7. Suk, K.T., H.S. Kim, M.Y. Kim, J.W. Kim, Y. Uh, I.H. Jang, S.K. Kim, E.H. Choi, M.J. Kim, J.S. Joo, and S.K. Baik, 2010. "In Vitro Antibacterial and Morphological Effects of the Urushiol Component of the Sap of the Korean Lacquer Tree (Rhus Vernicifera Stokes) on Helicobacter Pylori." *J Korean Med Sci*. 25(3):399-404.

8. Martin, Alain. 2010. North Cell Pharmaceutical, Inc. Phone and e-mail interviews.

9. Mohan, Jacqueline E., Lewis H. Ziska, William H. Schlesinger, Richard B. Thomas, Richard C. Sicher, Kate George, and James S. Clark. 2006. "Biomass and Toxicity Responses of Poison Ivy (Toxicodendron Radicans) to Elevated Atmospheric Carbon Dioxide." PNAS (*Proceedings of the National Academy of Sciences*) 103(24).

COMMERCIAL PRODUCTS

This is **not** a list of recommended products. It is an informational list of many poison oak and poison ivy rash products for sale. Some of them are full of natural herbal extracts and some are full of chemicals (which doesn't necessarily mean they're toxic, but they could be). If a product you are familiar with is not included, I may have missed its name in my search, considered it completely worthless—or, as in the case of a couple of Internet companies with lots of bells and whistles, I was suspiciously unable to reach anybody who could answer my questions.

At least two small company owners suspected I was their competition trying to wrest secrets from them. Another was incensed when I doubted a harebrained theory he had made up as to why his formula supposedly worked. Science didn't influence him. He replied that all scientists are jerks.

One big problem with commercial (and homemade) remedies is that something will work wonders for one person and do absolutely nothing for another. Besides individual differences, the products might be not be used as intended. A barrier cream could be applied too thinly, an oil remover scrub might miss the spots where the allergenic oil actually is, and an anti-itch cream not used often enough will be ineffective.

All Terrain Poison Ivy/Oak Bar

All Terrain is a small company with "Natural remedies for outdoor enthusiasts." The soap bar has no harsh ingredients, but should do the job of removing poison oak and poison ivy oil. Tea tree oil, neem oil and oat extract ingredients also help sooth irritated, itchy skin. The bar comes with a carrying case, convenient for putting in your hiking pack.

www.allterrainco.com • 800.246.7328

Anti-Itchy

This product, available in a one-ounce spray bottle, sooths itchy skin. Formulated by two Ayurvedic consultants, it is full of great healing and anti-itch herbs, The active ingredients are calendula, mugwort, Dead Sea salts, apple cider vinegar and natural menthol crystals. Also included are aloe vera; evening primrose oil; sea buckthorn berry; and essential oils of tea tree, lavender, Virginia cedarwood, geranium, carrot seed, juniper, roman chamomile, blue chamomile, and helichrysum. It has a pleasant herbal scent and the oils feel good on your skin.

www.antiitchy.com • 877.999.1360

Aveeno Skin Relief Bath Treatment

Aveeno brand has been around for a long time. You can probably find it in any pharmacy. The company has a number of skin products, but Skin Relief Bath Treatment is the one most often mentioned for poison oak and poison ivy itch relief. Finely ground oats float in a "milky dispersion" to coat and soothe itchy skin. This treatment is helpful in the evening when you have a light or medium rash in numerous spots and want to soak and relax in something soothing before you retire.

www.aveeno.com

Bodyguard

Bodyguard was developed by Alphacura Labs, a small company in northern California. Its ingredients are all botanical and completely safe. A fire chief at the State Department of Forestry wrote a letter of high praise after observing staff using Bodyguard all summer. Bodyguard is formulated from a root extract. The listed ingredients are actually from the extract: beta-D glucoside, arginine, stigma-sterol. Aloe vera is added as a carrier into the skin, and vitamin C as a stabilizer.

Bodyguard is a healer, not a barrier or oil remover. It is not designed to deal with dangerously serious rashes. Use it for mild to somewhat severe cases. As an extra benefit, the product has strong antifungal qualities.

www.poisonoaks.com   •   888.528.7346

Burt's Bees Poison Ivy Soap

These products are pretty well-known within the natural products crowd—and yes, Burt was once a beekeeper. The company is ecologically conscious. The featured ingredient in the bar soap is pine tar. Sounds terrible, but it's an old folk remedy for soothing skin afflictions, plus it's antiseptic. Jewelweed, a plant popular in the east for poison ivy rashes, is included, along with kaolin clay and soothing oat kernel protein—all in a vegetable soap base. Besides washing the oil from the skin, the bar is designed for leaving the lather on your rash two to three times a day to help relieve itching and irritation.

www.burtsbees.com   •   800.849.7112

Caladryl

Calamine is the main ingredient in this pink lotion. The second active ingredient is primoxine HCL to numb the skin (not likely). There are about 11 inactive ingredients, about eight of which are chemicals.

• **Caladryl Clear** is an anti-itch lotion without calamine. It contains heaps of chemicals. The active ones are pramoxine HCL (numbs skin) and zinc acetate (anti-itch, and also used in nutritional supplements).

www.caladryl.com   •   800.223.0182

Calamine Lotion

You can buy calamine lotion without toxic ingredients if you look at the labels. Rite Aid, for example, markets a calamine lotion with bentonite (clay), calcium hydroxide, glycerin and water. Calamine is a mixture of zinc oxide with a little bit of ferric oxide. The FDA considers calamine to be effective in treating poison ivy. Although it is marketed as an anti-itch skin soother, when the pink liquid evaporates, a powder is left to sop up weeping blisters. It does become messy--just lovely on your face. By the way, some people get an itchy rash from using calamine and think their poison ivy rash is sticking around.

Cordless Hair Dryer

This suggestion is for the seriously allergic individual who needs help to stop the itch when away from home and there is no available electricity. The Helpful Heat Technique For Itch Relief as taught in this book will stop the itch for up to seven hours. A hair dryer is the best way to apply the heat needed.

There are at least two cordless hair dryers on the market from one company. Charge it on the base and get about eight minutes on high heat. Take it with you during the day for touch-ups on your rash. You need only about 20 seconds on a pretty good-sized area. I found some on Amazon.com and eBay.com. The price is (gulp!) $129 or $139. Google "cordless hairdryer" on the Internet.

Cortaid

Cortaid is a division of Johnson & Johnson. Don't expect "natural." This is a company that uses chemicals to do the job.

• **Cortaid Poison Ivy Care Toxin Removal Cloths.** The 8" x 7" toxin removal cloths are pre-moistened and individually packaged. Wipe the affected area, and either use water or a dry cloth to rinse off the product. The honeycomb texture of the cloth is designed to trap the oil that has been bound and surrounded. The individually wrapped removal cloths are more expensive per wipe, but they would be very handy for hiking.

• **Cortaid Poison Ivy Care Treatment Kit (Removal Scrub and Treatment Spray).** The granules in the removal scrub help dislodge the plant resin that contains the allergenic oil. Like the removal cloths, the ingredients were chosen to bind with and surround the allergenic oil urushiol. Clinical results on more than 80 people showed that, compared with no treatment, the scrub and the cloth removed 95% of the allergenic oil from the skin.

www.cortaid.com

Dermisil

• **Dermisil Poison Ivy Cure.** Jojoba oil is the base for this all-natural essential oil formula. The ingredients are chosen for their anti-inflammatory, healing, antibacterial, soothing and drying abilities. Ingredients include lemon grass, tea tree, lavender, euca-lyptus, and patchouli.

• **Dermisil Sulfur Lavender Soap.** Sulfur has a strong drying effect. It will help dry up the poison oak and poison ivy rash. Other ingredients create a soothing medicinal bar.

   This small company is growing quickly. Products can be found in Walgreens (phar-macies) and Whole Foods (natural food stores).

www.dermisil.com (don't mistakenly type "dermasil" with an "a", because it will take you to the wrong company) • 888.371.2499

Domeboro Astringent Solution (Burrow's Solution)

This is a popular product from Bayer. Make a solution of the packet and soak the af-fected area for 15 to 30 minutes. The ingredients aluminum sulfate tetradecahydrate and calcium acetate monohydrate, when combined, create aluminum acetate. Although this product has been sold for many years, Internet sites caution that the chemical can cause sloughing of the skin from prolonged exposure, and is toxic if ingested.

www.bayercare.com

Electronic Itch Stopper

This seems to be a small company. The product is a handheld device with a metal plate a bit larger than a quarter. It becomes hot, but not enough to burn. Holding it on the rash will produce heat, which I believe is actually why it works (see the chapter on THE HELPFUL HEAT TECHNIQUE), but *they* say it "temporarily stops the degranulation process of skin mast cells, which will stop the histamine release." The heat produced is not enough for extended itch relief, but it does help stop itch for a while. With rashes on multiple spots, it will take some time to make the rounds, though. Luckily it comes with a power cord because, if you don't have rechargeable batteries, alternatively using it with six AA batteries could be expensive. The price is around $60.

www.itchstopper.com • 800.881.2933

Fels-Naptha Bar Soap

People keep talking about the old Fels-Naptha. It contained Stoddard solvent (mineral spirits), a petrochemical skin and eye irritant. Sure it cut oil. It's not the same soap now, although Dial keeps advertising it as the good ol' Fels-Naptha. Now it's a lye soap made from tallow—along with lots of other additives, even chemical colors.

www.felsnaptha.com

Gloves in a Bottle (Barrier Product)

A man who works every once in a while with oriental lacquerware, doing repair with the resin from the Japanese lacquer tree (almost identical to poison oak and poison ivy resin), told me he uses this product to protect his hands from contamination. Artists find it helpful while using oil paints. It is advertised as a "shielding lotion" and bonds with the outer layer of skin, wearing off as skin cells die. If you need just hand protection, this will work, but I wouldn't cover a large amount of skin area.

www.glovesinabottle.com

Goop

I'm not talking about the original Goop, containing mineral spirits, that was originally designed for removing auto grease and dirty oil. This is their new, more "natural" product. It's a powerful oil remover. They still produce the old product, so look for an orange bottle with the words "Orange Goop. Pumice Hand Cleaner." It has a big picture of an orange slice. The product contains two of my favorite resin and oil removers, limonene and pumice. It's biodegradable. Don't use water until you are ready to rinse. It's in lots of stores besides auto supply. This is a small, family-owned company.

www.goophandcleaner.com • www.momsgoop.com

Herb Pharm Soothing Oak & Ivy Compound

Herb Pharm is a small company in southern Oregon, but well-known in the herbal market. This herbal tincture has an earthy smell of herbs and natural menthol, which I like. It goes on as a liquid and dries to a very thin glaze that continues to keep the skin feeling protected from drying out as the rash heals, rather than feeling dry and prickly as some other remedies I tested do. It also is a psychological boost when you can tell the remedy is still there. It contains grindelia, sassafras, natural menthol crystals, grain alcohol, glycerine, and water.

www.herb-pharm.com • 541.846.6262

Hyland's Poison Ivy/Oak Tablets

These tablets are a traditional homeopathic formula for the relief of symptoms after contact with poison ivy or poison oak. It is safe for adults and children. The ingredients are a homeopathic dilution of poison ivy oil, and purging croton and bear grass plants.

www.hylands.com • 800.624.9659

Ivarest

• **Ivarest Medicated Poison Ivy Cleansing Foam.** The cleansing foam is touted as a cleanser of the allergenic oil, plus an itch soother and pain reliever. It contains lots of menthol (chemical, not natural), a short-lived cooling and anti-itch agent. Gently rub and rinse with water and the cleansers will wash the oil away.

• **Ivarest Poison Ivy Itch Cream.** This cream contains an antihistamine, Benadryl (diphenhydramine), which is not considered to be beneficial topically. Some people also develop allergies to it. Fourteen percent of the formula is calamine. I found straight calamine to be quite messy, so you could try this product when blisters are seeping to see how it works when added to a cream. There also are about 22 other ingredients, most of which are chemicals.

www.blistex.com • 800.837.1800

Ivy Block (barrier product)

This product has been clinically tested and deemed very satisfactory in blocking the allergic oil from your skin. It was formulated by well-known poison oak researcher William Epstein in the 1980s. The homeopathic company, Hylands, markets the product. It is a lotion, containing bentoquatam, a modified bentonite clay that has an even more oil absorbing abilitiy than regular bentonite clay. A special formula keeps it from drying out and falling off.

www.ivyblock.com • 800.991.DERM

Ivy Dry

• **Ivy Dry Defense (barrier product).** This is a sunscreen with a waterproofing agent, including a zinc compound acting as a barrier to the allergenic oil of poison oak and poison ivy. I didn't see the study, but a company spokesperson related that a small clinical test came out 100% positive on 12 people who were allergic to poison oak and poison ivy and who did not react on the arm on which Ivy Dry Defense was applied.

• **Ivy Dry Bar Soap.** There are three little soap bars in the box, the size of hotel soaps. I like that they take up little space in your hiking pack. You can keep a bar in the glove compartment, in your overnight kit, etc. The bars contain nonoxynol-9, which is thought to actually pull the allergenic oil out of the skin after it has started to be absorbed into the lower layers.

This soap is gentle enough to use on your entire body, yet contains effective soaps for washing the oil away. Oat flour and aloe are soothing to the skin. Tiny plastic balls help dislodge the oil from the skin.

• **Ivy Dry Scrub.** This is a gel scrub, a detergent-based product that contains nonoxynol-9 like the bar soap. The company says it is an "evolution of the old Lava and Fels

Naptha soaps concept with improved, more urushiol targeted detergents." Aloe vera and vitamin E are added to promote healing.

• **Ivy Dry Super.** This is a drying agent containing four active ingredients for itch: zinc acetate, benzyl alcohol, camphor, and menthol and benzyl alcohol. It's a liquid in a spray bottle.

• **Ivy Dry Cream.** This cream contains the same ingredients as Ivy Dry Super without the alcohol.

www.ivydry.com • 800.443.8856

Marie's Original Poison Oak Soap

I spot this herbal bar soap, formulated by Marie, all over the Internet stores and in the natural food store where I live. It contains clay and oat bran, both of which help to gently scrub the allergenic oil from the skin. Other ingredients are betula lenta, salix alba, morinda citrifolia, sassafras albidum, and grindelia, one of the best-known poison oak and poison ivy itch soothers—meaning that this bar also is designed to help sooth itchy skin.

www.poisonoaksoap.com • 845.352.9187

Oral Ivy

This product was designed to give seasonal resistance to poison oak and poison ivy. A clinical study found Oral Ivy to be effective after 455 allergic people who were normally exposed to the allergenic plants were given the product before spring, and then were studied during the summer. Seventy-seven percent either had no rash after normal exposure or, if so, experienced far less than normal outbreaks.[97]

The solution is a homeopathic dilution, containing minute parts of the allergenic oil. The dose is "5 drops in 1/4 glass of water or juice daily by mouth 1 or 2 weeks before exposure and continuing throughout the poison oak and poison ivy season." You can also take the product every day or so indefinitely for year-round resistance. The bottle contains 5 ounces, so it will last a good while.

The brochure says that homeopathic medicines are known for their safety and absence of side effects. Besides helping to develop a seasonal tolerance, Oral Ivy may be given *during* a rash to ease symptoms.

The family of the man who formulated the dilution in the late 1930s still distributes the product.

www.oralivy.com • 800.553.6778

Paradise Road Soap Company

This is an organic, all-natural soap made by a husband-and-wife team Steven and Karen in California. They created the recipe after being frustrated by Steven's continual allergic reactions to poison oak. Forestry officials and workers started using and liking the soap, and a business was born. Vegetable glycerin, a gentle-yet-strong soap is the base. Essential oils are added, along with bits and pieces of mugwort. You also are encouraged to use the soap for soothing an existing rash. The bar has its own recyclable case.

www.poisonoakandivysoap.com • 805.691.1005

Redmond Trading Company

• **Bentonite Clay.** I talk about clay numerous times in this book as a quick, dry scrub to pull the allergenic oil from your skin, to rub on a rash to sop up blister oil, and as a wet poultice to help heal an angry rash, especially if it is becoming infected. Redmond is a small, family-owned company. I buy clay from them, add water and eat a little each day for the minerals.

www.redmondclay.com • 800.367.7258

Tecnu

One of the main companies mentioned on web discussion groups, Tec Laboratories produces five products. The first two I discuss are the most popular. Tecnu Original was the first one developed and has been around for a long while. It is strictly an oil remover. Tecnu Extreme is an oil remover with anti-itch and anti-burning capabilities.

• **Tecnu Original Outdoor Skin Cleanser.** This product is a skin cleanser designed to remove radioactive dust, but the inventor's wife discovered it was very effective in removing poison oak oil as well. Apply up to eight hours after exposure to remove contaminants from the skin. Rinse with water. It contains mineral spirits (considered less toxic than other petroleum distillates), propylene glycol, octylphenoxy-polythoxethanol, mixed fatty acid soap, and fragrance. A number of people have told me they always us this when they have been contaminated by poison oak or poison ivy oil.

• **Tecnu Extreme Medicated Poison Ivy Scrub.** Although it does not contain mineral spirits, this product is designed to both remove the oil (tiny plastic beads help) and treat the rash. For *both* jobs you add water to the gel in your palm, gently scrub the skin, and rinse with water. Ingredients are grindelia robusta 3x (homeopathic), benzethonium chloride, carbomer, cocamide DEA, fragrance, polyethylene beads, polyoxyethylene (4) lauryl ether, polysorbate 20, purified water, and SD alcohol 40B.

• **Tecnu Rash Relief.** A medicated spray, this is a homeopathic formula consisting of grindelia robusta, plantago major, and alcohol. The label says "stops itching and pain. Dries oozing. Promotes healing."

• **Calagel.** Tec Labs say this is a "hydrocortisone-free antihistamine gel." Topical ingredients are benzethonium chloride, diphenhydramine HCL, and zinc acetate. The gel disappears on your skin. My daughter gets minor poison oak rashes and says Calgel is all she needs.

• **Corticool.** A non-prescription product cannot contain more than 1% hydrocortisone, but Tec Labs says a study showed that their 1% cream Corticool penetrated 2.75% better than a 2.5% prescription cream. This is very weak medication, but if you apply any cortisone product, you need to continue until the end of the rash. If you stop, the rash could start anew.

Tec Laboratories has won numerous business awards, and is considered one of Oregon's best companies to work for.

www.teclabsinc.com • 800.482.4464

Zanfel

Removes allergenic oil, stops the itch, and heals the rash.

Zanfel is one of the two most-mentioned products on Internet poison oak and poison ivy discussion sites. Some people say it did nothing for them, but a high percentage call it fantastic. This product has very specific instructions for application. Follow the directions closely. To quote from the informative flyer in the box, "Zanfel's unique dual-action formula works to remove urushiol after symptoms begin and provides relief of itching within seconds of washing. Zanfel is effective at any stage of the allergic reaction." I tried it on a few people and the positive effect was immediate. It contains tiny plastic granules to assist in scrubbing the oil off the surface of the skin, but it is believed that the chemistry of the ingredients pull out allergenic oil that has already penetrated the skin, stopping or reducing a rash that has already begun to form. It's not cheap, but Zanfel fans don't care. Besides removing the allergenic oil and stopping the itch, Zanfel says "the rash will begin to subside within hours if the reaction is mild to moderate." A big positive is that there are "no known side effects or contraindications" from the ingredients, which are polyethylene granules, sodium lauroyl sarcosinate, nonoxynol-9, 12-15 pareth-9, disodium EDTA, quaternium-15, carbomer 2%, triethanolamine, and water.

Two clinical studies of Zanfel were conducted by the Emergency Medicine Program at St Luke's Medical Center, Bethlehem PA. One study in 2003 concluded that Zanfel "... when applied after exposure to urushiol, ameliorates [causes improvement] or prevents Toxicodendron-induced allergic contact dermatitis." A second study published in 2007 concluded that Zanfel "...is effective when used for treatment and post exposure prophylaxis of experimentally induced acute contact dermatitis..."

www.zanfel.com • 800.401.4002

GLOSSARY

Aerial roots: Roots exposed to the air, usually anchoring the plant to a tree.

Allergen: A chemical substance that causes hypersensitivity (allergy) in a sensitized individual.

Anacardiol: The allergenic oil between the two layered shell of the cashew nut, called cashew shell oil.

Antigen: Foreign substance that induces an immune response in the body.

Antihistamine: Various compounds that counteract histamine in the body and are used to treat allergic reactions, although it is not effective for poison oak and poison ivy rash.

Antinflammatory: An agent that reduces inflammation

Automatic Sensor: The author's term for an automatic recognition avoidance response that slowly develops after you learn to identify poison oak and poison ivy plants.

Barrier product: When referring to poison oak and poison ivy, a substance that will act as a barrier between the allergenic oil, and the skin.

Cashew nut shell oil: The allergenic oil from the honeycombed space between the two layers of the cashew nut shell.

Compound leaf: A leaf composed of a number of leaflets on a compound stalk.

Contact dermatitis: Skin reaction from contact with an allergen or irritating substances.

Corticosteroid: Various steroids (hormones) of the adrenal cortex. Used medically as anti-inflammatory agents by reducing the effectiveness of the immune system.

Cortisone: A corticosteroid hormone, normally produced by the adrenal gland.

Cross-reaction: An allergic reaction to a substance chemically related to the original sensitizer.

Desensitivity: When sensitivity of an allergic person to the allergen has been reduced.

Drupes: Fleshly fruit with a thin skin and one central stone containing the seed. Cherries, eg.

Epidermis: Outer layer of skin. It is composed of four layers.

Female flower: Produces seeds, but no pollen.

Gall: Pouch-like reddish growths, created by the plant after gall mites layed their eggs in the plant tissue.

Ginkgolic acid: Allergenic oil in parts of the ginkgo tree, mainly in the pulp of the fruit.

Hapten: A allergen of low molecular weight, that has combined with Langerhans cells in the epidermis and is ready to be presented to T cells.

Hardening: A term used when an individual notices a decrease in reaction from exposure to poison oak or poison ivy oil.

Helpful Heat Technique for Itch Relief: The author's term for applying heat to a poison oak or poison ivy rash; hot enough to be uncomfortable, but not hot enough to burn the skin. The purpose is to stop the itch for up to seven hours.

Hermaphrodite: A plant (or animal) having both male and female reproductive systems.

Histamine: An immune system chemical that causes the release of chemicals that cause skin inflammation.

Hypoallergenic: Reduced ability to cause allergy.

Hypersensitivity: Allergy.

Itch receptors: Nerve network in the skin that causes an urge to scratch.

Lacquer: In this book, the term refers to the resin of the Japanese lacquer tree *T. vernicifluum* after it has been processed. It is painted on various types of objects to produce lacquerware.

Lacquerware: A decorative article painted with urushi, the processed resin from the Japanese Lacquer tree *T. vernicifluum*.

Ladder fuel: A plant that burns easily, assisting the spread of fire up tree trunks.

Langerhans cells: Immune system cells that bind to urushiol in the first part of an allergic reaction.

Latex: A compound produced in special cells (laticifers) of certain plants (rubber tree eg.).

Leaflet: Part of a compound leaf. Poison oak and poison ivy generally have three leaflets per leaf.

Limonene: Liquid from pressed orange peels. A cleanser and oil remover.

Lipid: Fat-like molecule that does not dissolve in water.

Lymph: The fluid that flows between body cells (interstitial fluid). An important part of the immune system, it drops off needed material, and picks up debris.

Lymphocyte: a white blood cell that mediates the immune reactions. Langerhans and T cells, eg.

Male flower: A flower that produces pollen but no seeds.

Noxious stimulation: In the case of poison oak and poison ivy, uncomfortable or painful stimulation to the skin that affects the nerve network to reduce or stop itch.

Opposite leaf pattern. When leaves are alternate on a stem instead of being right across from each other.

Oxidize: To combine with oxygen.

Patch test: A test to determine allergic sensitivity by applying small pads soaked with allergen to the unbroken skin.

Petiole: Leaf stem.

Petrochemical: Any compound obtained from petroleum or natural gas.

Polymerization: Chemical compounds made of small, identical molecules linked together, forming polymers.

Pregnisone: A synthetic corticosteroid drug, effective as an immune system suppressant. It is often used for serious poison oak and poison ivy allergic reactions.

Pumice: Finely ground volcanic rock.

Resin: a sticky compound flowing in special canals inside the bark of certain shrubs and trees for defense when bark is pierced.

Rhizome: Fleshly root; actually underground stem. New plants sprout as the rhizome spreads.

Sap: Water with dissolved sugars and mineral salts in a plant. The two types of cells carrying the liquid are xylem and phloem.

Sensitization: Relating to allergy, the first exposure to an antigen that sets the stage for symptoms of allergy upon the next encounter.

Sensitized: Having developed an allergy to an antigen (poison oak oil e.g.)

Solvent: Liquid substance capable of dissolving or dispersing one or more other substances.

T cells: Lymphocytes from the thymus gland, part of the immune system. They participate in a variety of immune reactions.

Tincture: Medicinal herbs are soaked in alcohol, vinegar or glycerin for two weeks and then strained.

Tolerant: An individual who was never exposed to a particular allergen, or who did not develop sensitivity upon exposure to the allergen.

Urushi: The resin of the Japanese lacquer tree *T. vernicifluum.*

Urushiol: General term for a group of related compounds in the plant genus *Toxicodendron* that causes a delayed allergic dermatitis (rash).

Volatile: An oil that vaporizes readily.

Vaporize: To convert (as by the application of heat or by spraying) into vapor.

INDEX

ABOUT THE AUTHOR

Sandra lives in the southern Oregon hills on five acres carpeted by poison oak with her husband and a succession of rescue dogs. She wrote a small book on poison oak and poison ivy in 1979.

CPSIA information can be obtained
at www.ICGtesting.com
Printed in the USA
BVHW091729301220
596742BV00003B/354

9 780983 370604